THE

PERSONAL ECONOMIC MODEL

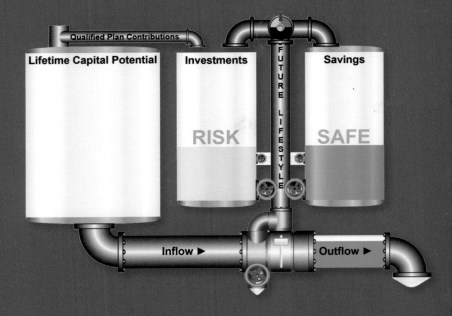

There is more money to be had
by avoiding the losses than
in trying to pick the winners!

THE
PERSONAL ECONOMIC MODEL

DON BLANTON / DR. C.W. COPELAND

The Personal Economic Model
ISBN: 978-0-9836814-4-1
Copyright © 2018 by
Don Blanton / Dr. C.W. Copeland
381 Santa Rosa Blvd
Ft. Walton Beach, Florida 32548

Published by
Alliance Publishing, LLC
P.O. Box 190405
Birmingham, AL 35219

Printed in the United States of America

The Personal Economic Model Chapters

Dedication

I would like to dedicate this book to the tens of thousands of men and women with whom I have been privileged to speak and train over the last 25 years of my career in the financial services industry. There is a great deal of truth in the statement that the teacher learns more than the student and it is certainly true in my case. In addition to sharing ideas to help advisors better serve their clients I have taught each one that "Wisdom, Without Compassion, is Arrogance."

Advancements in technology and the tremendous impact of the computer have provided opportunities to improve almost every area of our lives including our access to financial information. Trying to bring clarity to a subject that can seem very complicated and make it easier to understand has been my goal and mission from the first day I started my company.

As I have traveled the country training advisors on how to communicate on a higher level with their clients about finances I have received more value from them than they perhaps have received from me. Responding to their comments and questions about how to use the financial software my company developed has given rise to many of the concepts and information you will read in this book.

Although I can't list each and every name of the thousands of advisors who have impacted my life and thoughts, I want to dedicate this book to them. It would be arrogant of anyone to take credit for something that has been freely given to them.

A special thank you to the Circle of Wealth family of advisors.

Don Blanton   *a.k.a. Don Buddy*

Introduction

"A picture is worth a thousand words."
You have probably heard this famous English idiom. It refers to the notion
that a complex idea can be conveyed with just a single still image or that an
image of a subject conveys its meaning or essence more effectively than a
description can ever do.

It was first coined by Fred Barnard on December 8th in 1921 in an advertising campaign on the side of street cars. He later told people it was a famous
Chinese proverb so that people would take it seriously. The public bought
into the idea and credited Confucius with its origination. The actual Chinese
saying is, "hearing something 100 times is not better than seeing it once."

No matter how you heard it, the meaning is easily understood.

Imagine a picture that helps you understand how money really works –
how certain financial products play a role in solving your challenges, how
they work together to impact your personal finances. Hearing or reading
about how money works increases our level of understanding, but seeing how
it works cements an indelible image in our mind and moves our level of
understanding to a higher level.*

When I first shared this picture, I was often asked how long it took to
develop this powerful communication tool and I responded 100 days. Actually it was twenty years and 100 days. It took the first twenty years of my
career to learn what I needed to know to be able to wake up one day and "see"
the picture of the Personal Economic Model before I could draw the picture.

In the continued pursuit of trying to help clients better understand the
complex and difficult nuances of the multitude of financial products available
and more importantly how those products impact both your current and
future lifestyle, the Personal Economic Model (PEM) was born.

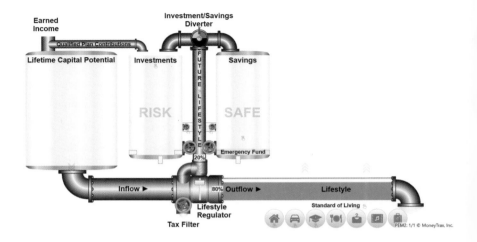

At first glance, it does not look like much more than something you might see in the basement or mechanical room of your home. You quickly notice a series of tanks—and tubes connecting the tanks—labeled with terms that convey something to do with money.

The Personal Economic Model or PEM is a cash flow picture of what happens to your money.

Let's begin with a simple question: What do you want your financial future to look like?

Let me make it even easier. Finish this sentence:

I want my future standard of living and lifestyle to be...

A: better than it is today.

B: at least the same as it is today.

or C: worse than it is today.

If you are like most people, you probably answered (A) or (B), but never (C).

So let's use the picture to explain your answer.

On the left side of the model, you will notice a big tank labeled Lifetime Capital Potential. This large tank represents the fact that you will earn a lot of money during your lifetime through your earned income. While a great deal of money comes into this tank, no money actually accumulates in it. Every dollar drops to the bottom and flows through the Monthly Cash Flow Tube unless you have arranged to defer some of your income to your retirement on a pretax basis in a retirement savings accounts called Qualified Plans. (More on Qualified Plans in chapter 5 and 16)

The next stop is called the Tax Filter, installed by the federal and local governments. Every dollar you earn must pass through this filter at some point. You can send money to the Investment Tank through the Qualified Plan Contribution Tube avoiding the tax filter today to be taxed at the time of withdrawal. All other dollars must pass through the Tax Filter before you can save or spend them.

Once through the Tax Filter, your money arrives at a very important place in the model called the Lifestyle Regulator. It regulates the amount of flow into the Savings and Investment Tanks with the balance flowing on through to your current lifestyle to be spent on your lifestyle expenses. Your future lifestyle depends on how much you pump into your Savings and Investment Tanks and how well you manage those dollars along the way.

So let's get back to the question I asked you earlier. What do you want your future lifestyle and standard of living to look like? It should be obvious that if you are going to live the same or better in the future than you do today you will need to find a balance between the money you spend on your current lifestyle desires and the money you put away for your future lifestyle requirements.

Understanding the Personal Economic Model will help you design a plan to live life today to the fullest while keeping in mind what you need to do to secure your future lifestyle. Getting your financial life together takes thought and discipline which many consider painful. Understand that you will experience pain to get your finances in order but it will also be painful if you do nothing. It has been said there are two types of pain: the pain of discipline and the pain of regret. It is up to you to choose which of the two types of pain you want to live through.

There are only two ways to improve your present financial position. The first is to find better financial products that offer the potential to pay higher rates of return but often require more risk. The second is to be more efficient by avoiding unnecessary losses.

This book will not focus so much on where to put your money but seeks to help you better understand and navigate the turbulent waters of the financial world with solid financial information so that you can be more efficient. Our goal is to show you where you can find dollars you may be losing unnecessarily to balance your current lifestyle desires and your future lifestyle requirements without impacting your present standard of living.

We believe "There is more to be gained by avoiding the losses than picking the winners."

Chapter 1:
The Parts and Function of the Personal Economic Model

N ow that you have a brief understanding of the model, let's take a deeper look at each of the components to learn how they interact with one another. It is important that you understand each of the pieces of the model before we begin discussing how they work together.

Earned Income:

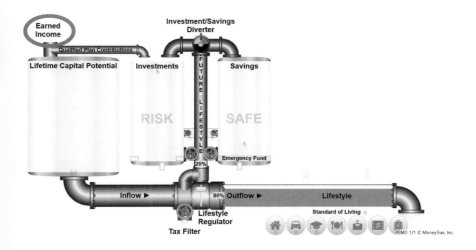

While there are several ways money gets into the model, the most significant entry point is most likely through earned income from your work or occupation. In addition to earned income from your occupation, you may have other sources of income such as an inheritance, Social Security, or investment income. We will look at investment income later when we discuss the Savings and Investment Tanks.

Many people count on their Social Security benefit when planning their financial future. Social Security benefits are taken as a tax when your earned income passes through the Tax Filter. Social Security tax dollars are taken from you today to pay benefits for those who qualify for benefits today. Many believe that their Social Security tax dollars are sitting in an account with their name on them waiting for their retirement. That is not so. The hope is that when you qualify to receive Social Security benefits, the taxes paid by others at that time will be sufficient to pay your benefit. There is no guarantee that there will be enough in the reservoir to pay benefits when it is your time to receive them.

If and when you receive a Social Security check, it must pass through the Tax Filter and could be taxed depending on your other earned income. Your Social Security benefit is not designed to be sufficient to replace the cash flow equal to the amount you are earning while working. If you are under the age of 50 it would be a prudent thing to plan as if you will not receive it and if you do, you will not be disappointed.

The amount of money you earn will have some degree of impact on the current lifestyle you enjoy today and the lifestyle you hope to enjoy during retirement. It is easy to get started on your financial journey ignoring the Savings and Investment Tanks and spend everything you make on your current standard of living with the belief that you have plenty of time to save for your future. Nothing could be further from the truth. The sooner you get started, the better off you will be.

Compound interest works best over time and uninterrupted. The road to your financial destination grows steeper and steeper the longer you postpone getting started.

Let me give you an example. Brandon starts saving $10,000 a year right out of college. His twin brother, Robert, decides to enjoy life now with the mindset to save later. Let's assume both average 6% over their lifetime on their savings. Brandon starts saving $10,000 a year from his current age of 25 till age 65. In 40 years he will have $1,640,477 at age 65. Robert waits until he is 40 to start saving, not knowing he will have to save $28,208 each year until he turns 65 to end up with as much money as his brother. If Robert saves $10,000 a year from age 40 to 65, he will only have $581,563.83. Compound interest needs time. The more time, the greater the compounding.

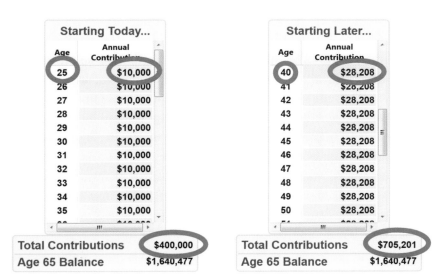

Starting Today...		Starting Later...	
Age	Annual Contribution	Age	Annual Contribution
25	$10,000	40	$28,208
26	$10,000	41	$28,208
27	$10,000	42	$28,208
28	$10,000	43	$28,208
29	$10,000	44	$28,208
30	$10,000	45	$28,208
31	$10,000	46	$28,208
32	$10,000	47	$28,208
33	$10,000	48	$28,208
34	$10,000	49	$28,208
35	$10,000	50	$28,208

Total Contributions	$400,000	Total Contributions	$705,201
Age 65 Balance	$1,640,477	Age 65 Balance	$1,640,477

NorL: 1/1 © MoneyTrax, Inc.

Notice that Robert will have to put away $705,201 of after tax dollars from his lifestyle while Brandon will only put away $400,000. Remember that the money they put away will require each of them to find a balance between how much they can spend now and how much they need to save for their future.

Human Life Value:

This may not be a term you have heard before, but it can help you gain a new perspective on your earned income as well as your lifetime capital potential. If you are ever involved in a wrongful death suit or accident caused by someone else that keeps you from being able to work, you will become very familiar with this concept.

Calculating your human life value is an effort to estimate the value of your financial life. It takes into consideration your current age, your potential retirement age, and your current income as well as the anticipated rate of inflation. It also considers the value of fringe benefits you and your heirs would have received had the accident not occurred. The value of your services to your family is also important because your family will need to spend money to replace the monetary value your loss imposes. Once the above things are considered, the amount of money for your self-maintenance in the event of a death would be subtracted. Had you lived, the amount necessary to cover your personal expenses is added to the equation. Finally, the amount necessary will include any tax obligations that would need to be met.

The purpose for the calculation is to help leave those left behind in the event of death or the party injured no better or worse financially. One way to look at this issue would be for you to consider what amount of money would you consider to be a fair settlement if you could never work again or your income potential was taken from your family?

Here are a few things to consider:

Why would you not have the same level of life insurance in force today that you would want your heirs to receive should your death should result from a wrongful death claim?

Why should your life be worth more when you are suing someone than the amount of coverage you have in force today?

What if you could only sue someone for the amount of coverage you had in force on your own life at the time of the accident?

Why should someone else place a higher value on your life than you believe your own life is worth demonstrated by the amount of protection you have in place today?

As you can see, when you do the calculation, your life is extremely valuable and the cost to replace your lifetime capital potential is significant.

Lifetime Capital Potential:

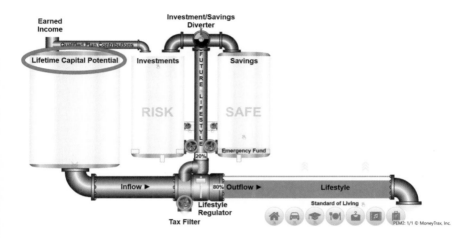

The importance of the big tank illustrated on the left side of the model is to signify that over your lifetime, you will have a great deal of money flow into and through this tank. You may not think you make much money, but when you consider the total dollars you will earn over your entire lifetime, it takes on a different meaning.

Let's suppose that on your first day on the job, you received a check for all the work you would do during your entire life. I understand that as you read that line your first thought was that you would never show up for work again. Now let me make a point. Let's say that check is $5,000,000 and you can't earn any other income and you can't earn any interest. You basically have an ATM machine in your house that you can take money from but can't put any more in. As you take money from the machine you would see your balance going down with each withdrawal. Would you look at that money differently than you look at the money you get each pay period? I am sure you would. The point is that you need to understand the value of every dollar you receive in order to make solid financial decisions that allow you to be as efficient as you can, avoiding unnecessary losses along the way. Since the money that will pass through your hands is finite, it demands that you maximize the use of every dollar.

Begin your financial planning with the end in mind. It is our desire for you to see your financial future from the beginning to the end as you study the Personal Economic Model. Knowing what you need to do today to ensure that you are prepared for the future will have a positive effect on your financial life, both today and tomorrow. The average American is not doing what they need to do to live like they live today in the future adjusted for inflation. If you wish to be financially where you want to be, you will need to do what others are not willing to do.

Monthly Cash Flow:

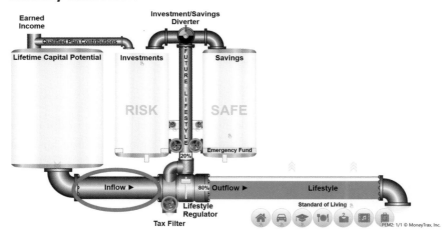

This is something that needs no explanation. Most of us live from month-to-month. Our fixed expenses are paid monthly and our discretionary spending is determined by how much we have left over after we have paid the bills. Most Americans do not receive their monthly cash flow until it has passed through the Tax Filter where the state and federal government have taken taxes due on their earnings. Most of us have taxes taken out of our payroll check, while others pay quarterly and some not until they are due on April 15th.

When thinking about your monthly cash flow, it is best to think of it in terms of after tax cash flow, your bring home pay after tax. When we get a job and they tell us what our gross annual salary will be, we don't really think in net terms that we will only get 70% or 80% depending on our tax rate. You may make a $100,000 but you can't live the lifestyle of someone who has $100,000. Remember that every dollar you earn must pass through the Tax Filter, which will reduce the amount of spendable income available. Not withholding taxes can cause a tremendous cash flow problem if the money is spent and you have nothing left to pay your taxes. The thing to consider is how much money you get to spend, not how much money you make.

Remember that you have a partner, meaning the federal government that must be paid before you have any money to spend. There is a penalty for not paying your taxes. It is five years in the federal pen. The tax law requires you to pay what is owed but no more.

The Tax Filter:

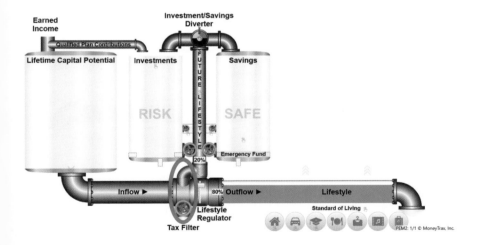

If you focus your attention on the copper Tax Filter, you will notice it takes center stage in the model. Every dollar will eventually flow through the Tax Filter where the federal and state governments can extract the money they require to handle their operating expenses and civic responsibilities. There is an option to avoid paying taxes initially on income coming into the model through contributions to qualified retirement plans where the government allows you to postpone your taxes until your retirement to be taxed when you withdraw the money. We will cover qualified plans in detail in Chapters 5 and 17.

As you think about your money passing through the Tax Filter, how many times do you want it go through this part of your financial model? Some things you do require your money to pass only once, while others can require you to be taxed over and over every year. Minimizing unnecessary tax loss can have a big impact on your cash flow and your financial future. Details to follow in chapter's 4 and 16.

The Lifestyle Regulator:

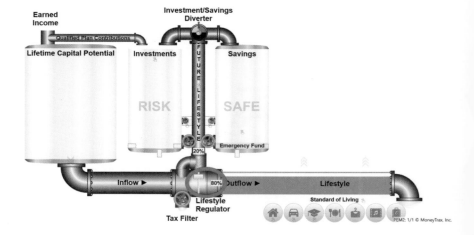

The Lifestyle Regulator may be the one piece of the model that plays the most important role of all in how you manage your money. It regulates the amount of money that you allow to flow through the regulator to your current lifestyle to be spent today and how much you pump up the Future Lifestyle Tube into your Savings and Investment Tanks to be spent in the future. Unlike the Tax Filter, this is a valve that you control. As you open the valve, it will allow more money to be consumed with your lifestyle expenses and as you close the valve, it will push money up the Future Lifestyle Tube into the Savings and Investment Tanks to be put away for your future. Your job is to balance your current lifestyle desires with your future lifestyle requirements. Many look to financial service professionals to help them manage their money which is a good thing especially if you have little skill in this area. Unfortunately many advisors are only concerned with helping you find a place to put your money rather than helping you with strategies to help you find money you may be losing unnecessarily. Some advisors only focus on the yellow tank or Investment Tank and some only on the green tank or Safe Tank.

It is important that you find an advisor that looks at your whole picture, including a key area which is protection. An analogy I like is that of the owner of a professional football team. The owner hires a head coach to build a winning team. It is the job of the head coach to oversee the entire operation and develop an overall philosophy on how to play the game. They

> **It is important that you find an advisor that looks at your whole picture, including a key area which is protection.**

hire offensive coaches, defensive coaches, and special teams coaches who understand his game plan and help him build a solid program.

You will need someone to handle the money in the Investment Tank to oversee your investment dollars who can maximize your return potential (Offense). You will also need an advisor to help you with the Safe Tank to help you move the ball down the field putting you in control of the game (Offense). Finally you will need special teams' coaches like your your Property and Casualty agent, CPA and attorney to make sure you have the proper protection in place with the right players on the field (Defense).

You should look to hire a head coach that can give you direction in every area of your financial model. It is not necessary or even probable that one person will be licensed to help you in every area we just mentioned. The head coach will usually have one or two areas they are experts in and will recommend the other coaches to help you. If they do not bring others to the table you can assume you have a coach who may be great in their area but you should continue looking for a head coach. While you are looking for a head coach, as the owner you should take an active role in understanding the head coaches game plan. Your job is managing the amount of flow through your Lifestyle Regulator. With a solid understanding of the Personal Economic Model, you will feel more confident when discussing recommended products and strategies suggested by the different coaches on your team.

Another valuable role the Lifestyle Regulator plays is that it will provide you with the answers to four questions you need to know to determine what you need to do today to be able to live like you desire in the future. The advisor who can help you with the answers to these questions is a good candidate for the head coaching position.

The four questions are:

1: Do you know what rate of return you will have to earn for you to be able to live in the future like you live today adjusted for inflation and have your money last to your life expectancy?
2: Do you know how much you should be saving each month or annually to make sure you will have enough set aside to live like you live today adjusted for inflation?
3: Do you know how long you will have to work before you can retire and have your money last to your life expectancy?
4: Do you know how much you will have to reduce your standard of living if you don't do something different to avoid running out of money before your life expectancy?

Obviously learning the answers to these four questions will give you the insight you will need to make better informed decisions about your finances. We will cover these questions in greater detail when we look at the application of the different pieces of the model.

Current Lifestyle Tube:

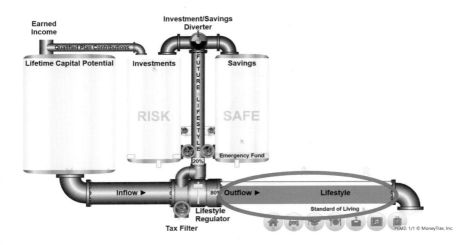

This tube supplies the cash flow necessary for you to pay for all the things that make up your standard of living. Those things include cars, house, education expenses for your children, food, clothing, vacations, entertainment and everything else we spend our money on that we call life. The key thing to walk away with about current lifestyle is that this is the natural flow for your money and any money that flows through this tube once spent it gone forever.

There is only one current lifestyle expense that has the potential to return money once spent and that is the money you spend to buy your house. Many consider the money in their house to be their best investment. We don't consider your house an investment because in order for you to have access to the equity, you would need to sell your house or borrow against it. You would then need to find another place to sleep. In order for you to make money where you sleep, you must be able to sell your house at a profit which is very difficult to do when you consider all related expenses, such as property taxes, homeowners insurance, and maintenance. When you factor in all the expenses you spend on where you sleep, you may have a new understanding of why we have your house listed as a lifestyle expense rather than an investment.

Your house and the decisions required to pay for it will most likely be your greatest single expense and is one of the top five areas where potential wealth transfers can occur unknowingly and unnecessarily. We will discuss mortgages in detail later in Chapter 15.

Future Lifestyle Tube:

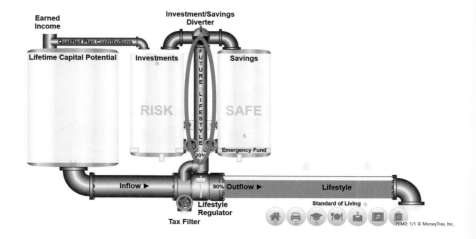

The Future Lifestyle Tube points upward to signify the fact that up is not the natural flow for your money. To put money away for your future you have to pump it into those tanks. It takes energy and effort which is much different than what it takes to satisfy your current lifestyle desires. Another concept you do not want to miss is the fact that in order to live in the future like you live today, you will need to balance your current lifestyle desires with your future lifestyle requirements. You can't spend everything you make and live that way forever. One day, you will not be able to work or you will choose not to work and your income at that time will depend on the money you have in your tanks to carry you financially through your life expectancy.

Learning how to balance how you live today with how you want to live in the future will reduce financial pressure in your model. The financial pressure you may be feeling today due to lack of access to money is not nearly as painful as if you retire with little or no access to capital and no way to earn more.

There is an important economic term you will need to understand and apply to every financial decision you make called opportunity cost. Opportunity cost represents the economic cost of every financial decision, factoring in what the dollars spent could have earned had they been saved and invested.

Let me give you an example. I have a friend who graduated from college this year. He bought a new Camaro and paid $25,000 in cash with money he had previously saved and the money he received from friends and loved ones upon his graduation. I introduced him to the concept of opportunity cost, something he had never heard of during his days on his college campus.

His $25,000 car cost him about $257,142. Had he saved the $25,000 and averaged a 6% rate of return during the next 40 years, when he turns 65, he could have had $257,142 in his account. The sticker price of the car was $25,000. The opportunity cost of the car was $257,142. He lost the potential of $257,142 from his lifetime capital potential. He likes his car but he sees it differently now.

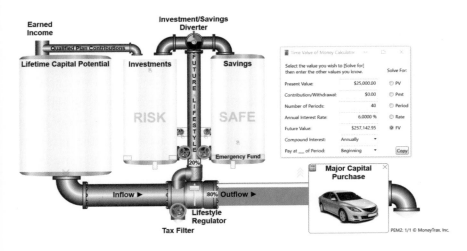

This does not mean he should not have purchased the car but rather, a new and more informed way of looking at money and the cost. Remember our lifetime capital potential discussion. The $25,000 spent today took $257,142 from his lifetime potential. Since the dollars we will earn are finite we need to look at them differently than we did before we understood opportunity cost.

We will get into the most efficient way to purchase cars later in chapter 14, Finance 101.

The Diverter Valve:

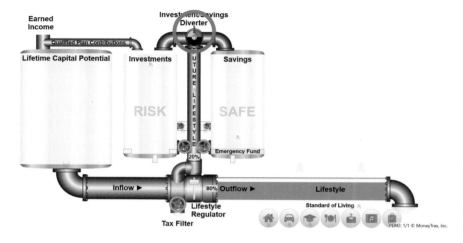

The Diverter Valve does exactly what you would think; it diverts the money you pump up the future lifestyle tube into your Savings and Investment Tanks. When it comes to how much should go into which tank, the percentage varies widely from one person to another and is a very personal decision. Some people have all their money in the investment tank with very little in the safe tank. Others are just the opposite, wanting no risk of losing even a dollar and others with every possibility in between the two just mentioned. There are many things that impact ones thinking on how much and what percentage should go into which tank. Age plays a very important role. The pendulum begins to swing from money in the Investment Tank, requiring risk, to the Safe Tank with little or no risk as we age. How much you make also plays a role, and of course, how you feel about risk is important as well.

The types of accounts in each tank will also be an important conversation as you think through the amount of money you want in which tank. You will need to develop your own thoughts on what percentage allocation makes the most sense to you. Your thoughts should not be one tank or the other but rather how much do you want in each tank. The power and freedom of access to capital in the Safe Tank is just as important as rate of return and the earnings potential in the Investment Tank. You should have money in both tanks, how much in which tank is up to you.

Safe Tank

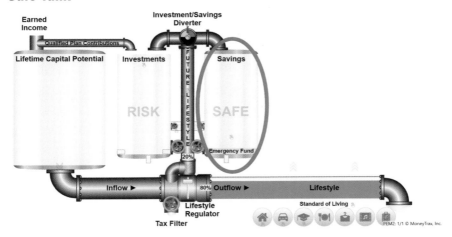

There are just a few things to think about with the Safe Tank. You will notice that the Safe Tank has a cap which signifies that money in this tank can't be lost. Obviously, low interest returns that do not keep up with inflation could be considered a loss over time but accounts in this tank are generally considered safe from the loss of principal. For example, CD account values in banks are guaranteed from loss of principal up to $250,000 by the FDIC.

Financial institutions often promote increased return opportunities on products by limiting accessibility. A good idea you have probably heard recommended by many advisors is that you should have a minimum of at least three to six months of your income set aside in an emergency fund account. The emergency fund account should be in the Safe Tank.

Another important feature of the Safe Tank is that money in this tank should be easily accessible. If all of your money is tied up in the investment tank with little to no access, you could be forced to borrow at exorbitant rates to cover an unplanned current lifestyle expense. Having little to no access to money in the time of trouble often leads to using credit cards to cover the expense. This is dangerous because while we may have every intention to pay it off quickly, sometimes things don't work out and we can end up losing by paying more interest on borrowed money than we are earning in our account that is inaccessible.

Access to capital also serves as the number one factor in reducing financial stress on the model when major capital purchases pop up from time to time. A major capital purchase is anything that you can't afford to pay for in full with monthly cash flow. Unfortunately, it is easy to find yourself with your money in the Investment Tank without access to capital because the main focus of these accounts is return not accessibility.

> **Unfortunately, it is easy to find yourself with your money in the Investment Tank without access to capital because the main focus of these accounts is return not accessibility.**

Little or no access to money causes stress and financial pressure. It is a situation we all understand and is all too common.

Investment Tank

The Investment Tank is a place to park assets and accounts that offer the opportunity for potentially higher returns than one would typically find in the Safe Tank. You will notice that there is no cap on the Investment Tank to signify that money can evaporate or be lost in this tank and one should carefully consider the risk of loss in any and every investment decision.

There is a myth floating around about money in the Investment Tank, which is that if you are young, you should be less concerned with risk because you have time to make up for a loss if one occurs. This type of thinking may be detrimental to your future financial success. The truth is that a loss is gone forever along with the opportunity of what those dollars could have been worth had you never lost them. A loss puts additional stress on the underlying investment to get back to the same position enjoyed before the loss. Greater return is certainly nice, but avoiding losses is our preferred recommendation to maximizing your wealth potential. It is easy to enjoy the increases but hard to forget the losses.

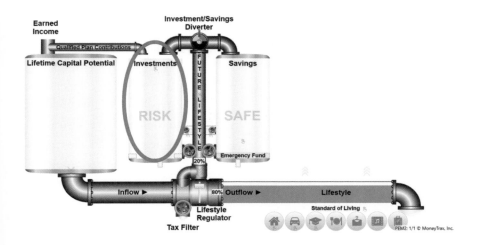

People get confused about the notion that it is possible to recapture money lost. It is not possible. In some ways, money is like time. You may have more time in the future, but you can't recapture the time you have lost. It is possible that you may be able to recoup or get back to or exceed your loss position, but you can never get the money lost back. The market may crash and you lose money, but if you stay around long enough for it to recover, you may get back to where you were before the loss. That is a different position than where you could have been had the loss never occurred.

You should also understand that many investment opportunities appreciate or depreciate over time but do not compound interest. Compound interest has been called the eighth wonder of the world, not appreciation. Compound interest over time, uninterrupted, now that is something to be desired.

Switch Valves:

Between the Savings and Investment Tanks you will notice a tube connecting the two tanks. This tube provides the ability to move money easily from one tank to the other. It also should help you understand that you have two tanks that work together rather than two independent tanks for your money.

Moving money from the Safe Tank to the Investment Tank is usually very easy because most of the dollars in the Safe Tank are very accessible. A reason to accumulate money in the Safe Tank is you need a certain amount to make a particular investment and you need a parking place until you have that amount. You would then move those dollars to the Investment Tank with the hopes for greater return potential.

Moving money from the Investment Tank to the Safe Tank depends on the type of account. Qualified plan dollars have restrictions on when you can have access to those dollars before age 59 ½ without taxes and penalties. Non-qualified accounts can be moved at your discretion but need not be moved in their entirety. Often one would chose to move the earnings from their investment to the Safe Tank for protection from loss and increased accessibility leaving the investment account to maximize their earnings potential.

> **Often one would chose to move the earnings from their investment to the Safe Tank for protection from loss and increased accessibility leaving the investment account to maximize their earnings potential.**

Distribution Valves:

These valves are designed to drain money from the two tanks, preferably in the future for your retirement years. Depending on the type of account in which your money resides, distribution rules will determine when and how you receive the money. When the valves are opened and the money must again flow through the Tax Filter. Remember that the Tax Filter is very sophisticated. It knows if the money has been through the filter before or not and if taxes have been collected or not. So even if the money has been through the filter before, it must again pass through the filter for the government to make sure it did not miss anything the first time before it gets to you.

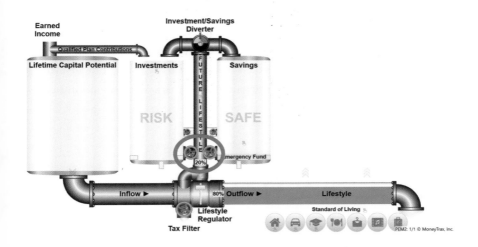

Some of your investment dollars may get into the investment tank through the Qualified Plan Contributions Tube postponing the taxes due until you open that valve. When you open the Distribution Valve, the government will take their share first of every dollar you withdraw from this account. You probably are wondering what tax rates will be when you take the money. That will depend on what amount of tax the government needs at the time you take it. If the tax rate when you take your money is higher than the rate you were at when you put it in, the government comes out ahead. If the tax rate when you take the money is lower than when you put it in, you get more. There is something you need to know about this arrangement. The IRS does not go back and ask what tax bracket you were in when you made the contribution. Their only concern is what your tax rate is at the time you take the money.

You may also have made contributions to the Investment Tank with after tax dollars, which are considered non-qualified because they do not "qualify" for tax deferral. As you earn interest, you could be taxed on the gain depending on the underlying account. There are some accounts that will allow you to defer the taxes on appreciating assets until you sell them. The same is true of interest earned in the Safe Tank. Interest earned in the Safe Tank contributed from after tax dollars is taxable. Since few people wish to see their account balance go down once they have seen it up, they choose to pay the taxes due from their current aftertax cash flow. This seems practical in the beginning when taxes due are low, but as the account grows, so do the taxes which can put a strain on dollars available needed to support current lifestyle. Few investment advisors will suggest you withdraw money from your investment account to pay the taxes due on the gains they are so proud to announce.

Standard of Living:

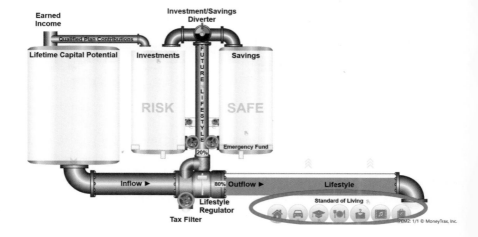

Your current lifestyle is directly proportional to the amount of after tax cash flow you have available to spend. The greater your spendable income, the greater your standard of living possibilities—the car you drive, where you live, the school your children attend, travel, food, clothing and entertainment.

None of us need any help in this area. Finding what to spend our money on is not very hard. I once heard someone say that it is not difficult to adjust your standard of living to more income but once tasted, it's almost impossible to adjust to less. Balancing our current lifestyle spending with the amount of money we should be saving does seem to cause issues. Unfortunately, many of us set our standard of living first before even knowing or understanding what is required to take care of our financial future.

The information you received from the Lifestyle Regulator made it clear that your current lifestyle is probably getting the lion share of your attention and your future lifestyle is on the back burner. I like to say there is a war at your house. It is the war between your current lifestyle desires and your future lifestyle requirements. Finding a workable balance is the position you should be trying to achieve in your personal economic model.

Balance is the key to your financial success, like it is in most things in life. We have all experienced times physically when we have been out of balance and losing our balance can be very dangerous. Being financially out of balance is also a dangerous position to be in. A balanced economic model would be one where you are putting away enough money to be able to live during your retirement like you live today adjusted for inflation and have enough money to live at a minimum until your life expectancy. The results from the Lifestyle Regulator provided you with the information you will need to find that balance—what rate of return you need, how much you should be saving, how long you will have to work, and if you do nothing, how much you will need to reduce your future lifestyle to avoid running out of money. For you to find the balance you desire, it may be necessary to make some changes in all four of those areas. You have options available to solve the shortfall, if necessary, if you start now and plan properly. Later in the book we will discuss opportunities to help you find money to help in the balancing dilemma without having to reduce your present standard of living.

This will not happen without planning and the discipline to stick to the plan. Besides managing the money you save and invest, you must also manage your standard of living. You can find an advisor to help you manage your money but you are going to have to manage your lifestyle. It is very easy to let our lifestyle desires get us in a position where we cannot put away the dollars needed for our future. At that point, we are making the decision that today is more important than tomorrow. When you dip into the money you already have saved for your future for a current lifestyle expense, in effect, you are robbing from your future. If you don't put the money back and at interest, you are again robbing from yourself. It should not surprise you that lifestyle is an insatiable appetite. There will always be someone with more than you and someone with something you want that you don't have that can cause you to lose your focus on what is important. Be careful; there are traps everywhere.

Time is also a factor which can cloud our thinking. Our nature is to believe we have plenty of time to solve our financial problems; so we ignore tomorrow and focus on the issues before us today. There will come a day when you will not have enough time or make enough money to find the balance we have been discussing and you could be forced to settle for less. We all could figure things out if we had more time but our time is finite. Developing a solid plan by first focusing on how to avoid unnecessary losses can help you make sure you have the best financial future possible with the resources you have available. Some people have enough money that the financial mistakes they make have little impact on their standard of living; however, there are very few in this category. The rest of the book will help you identify potential areas for loss and give you ways on how to avoid them, allowing you to solidify your financial future without having to reduce your present standard of living to do so.

When time seems to be running out, it tends to create even more stress and pressure to make up for the mistakes we have made along the way. Don't beat yourself up; we all make mistakes. Trying to solve your financial mistakes by taking on even more risk to earn greater returns could turn out to be a bigger mistake that those of the past. Focus first on what you can do to be more efficient before looking for the magic investment opportunity that will solve all your problems with higher returns.

The Foundational Role of Protection

There are basically eight areas of insurance protection you need to have in place in order to make sure that your current and future lifestyle are not interrupted by things outside your control. While none of these insurances move you closer to your financial future, they are vital because they keep you from going backwards. Most people look at insurance as a necessary evil, but take a minute and think about what life would be like without it. You may have said to yourself, "I am insurance poor." Imagine how poor you would be if you were unable to purchase insurance.

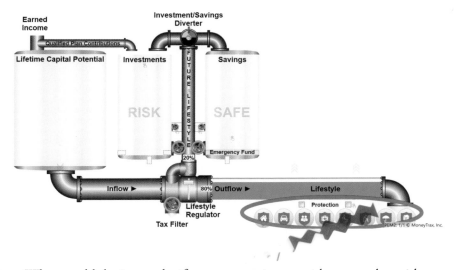

What would the impact be if your car was in an accident or stolen without auto insurance? How long would it take you to recover financially from a fire in your home? Insurance protects both your current as well as your future standard of living. Without it, you would constantly be draining your savings and investment tanks to cover losses and living in fear that at any time a catastrophic loss could occur that could bankrupt you. If something can take what you have from you, it is not really yours.

I am sure you are familiar with these forms of insurance but there are some things you should know about each that can keep you from suffering a loss unnecessarily. There are minimum levels of coverage and there are maximum levels in each of these areas below. As you accumulate more and more assets, your protection in these areas should increase as well.

Since none of these areas of protection move you forward financially, it is important that you concern yourself with not only making sure you have the coverage in place you want, but also managing the cost. None of the money spent on protection will ever return to you. The insurance is to keep you where you are, not move you forward. You can only buy protection to keep you from going backward if a loss should occur. Your job is to keep the ship moving forward, but having an anchor that can keep the current from pushing you backward is well worth the price.

When looking at protection, you need to understand the opportunity cost to have it compared to the opportunity cost if you don't. Remember what I said earlier. There is more opportunity in avoiding the losses than there is in picking the winners.

Chapter 2:
Human Life Value and Your Lifetime Capital Potential

What are you really worth? Your human life value is concerned about your worth from an economic position. You may be surprised to find out that you are worth much more than you may think.

The purpose for this discussion is to help you appreciate your own economic value and help you make prudent financial decisions to protect your true value and earning potential.

You may not be familiar with this concept; however, personal injury lawyers are faced with this question every day. Here in the United States, one is liable for doing harm to another and one's human life value aids the lawyers in determining the extent of that harm and validating a proper economic settlement in a wrongful death claim or an accident that left you or someone you harmed dead or unable to work.

Perhaps the best way to appreciate this concept is for you to consider the dollar amount you believe you would need financially to take care of you and your family should someone take your ability to work away from you. There are many factors that must be considered.

Your Current Age: Obviously, the younger you are the more years you would have had an opportunity to earn an income.

Your Retirement Age: Estimating how long you would have been able earn your income through your line of work is necessary to determine how many years of income you would have lost.

Your Current Income: How much you make today will play an important role in determining how much you would have made during your working years, had you been able to work.

Income Growth Potential: Like most people, it can be assumed that had you continued to work you would see increases in your income from raises due to the impact of inflation.

Value of Fringe Benefits: Perhaps you worked at a job that provided fringe benefits that will no longer be available to you if you can't work, such as major medical coverage, a car, and childcare. Benefits have an economic value and need to be considered in the total compensation.

Value of Services to Your Family: If you are not here or are incapacitated and you have to pay someone to do the things you once could do that now present an economic burden, this loss has a cost.

Percent Spent on Self Maintenance: In the event of death, the expense from these items will be subtracted. If you are injured and can't work and require ongoing medical care, that cost will be added to the amount of money needed to make you whole financially.

After-Tax Rate of Return: In most cases, the money received from a lawsuit come tax free to the recipient; however, any interest earned on money once received is taxable. It is important that the impact of taxes be considered to make sure an adequate income after taxes is just compensation.

There are two ways you should be looking at this information. The first, of course, is how you would want to be compensated in the event something happened to you and the second is what if you were the one who harmed someone else. Obviously, you would want you and your family to be compensated adequately. Should you accidentally harm someone else, they will seek to be compensated in the same fashion. It is important for you to have insurance in place so that you are covered, and the money you have worked so hard to put away for your future in your savings and investment tanks is not drained and taken from you by legal action. We will cover this topic in greater detail in the protection section in Chapter 12, but it is easy to see that your human life value is perhaps greater than you once thought and you can rest assured that when someone you have harmed has time to think about how much their ability to earn an income was really worth, you may be surprised at the value they place on their human life value as well.

The following calculation represents the human life value of someone with the following inputs. As you can see, it is over $2,000,000. This gives the attorneys a starting point to begin their negotiations. Looking at your income from this point of view should give you a new appreciation for your income and how important it is for your family, if you can't earn a paycheck.

Human Life Economic Value

Current Age	42
Retirement Age	65
Current Income	$102,000
Income Growth	3.00%
Value of Fringe Benefits	$5,000
Value of Services to Family	$3,000
% Spent on Self-Maintenance	10.00%
After-Tax Rate of Return	4.00%

Your human life economic value is $2,068,201

This is the estimated lump sum needed to replace the lifetime income and services you provide for your family, based on the assumptions above.

HLEV: 1/1 © MoneyTrax, Inc.

Income and Wealth Potential, Opportunity Cost and Time Value of Money

While your human life value focuses on your income potential that may be lost or taken, your wealth potential looks at your future income from a more positive viewpoint. The big tank on the left of the PEM model represents the fact that you are going to have a great deal of money flow through your hands over your lifetime.

The point this conversation is making is that while you will have a lots of money flow through your hands, it is a finite amount. No matter how much you make, it is not unlimited. Limited or finite suggests that one day, your ability to earn an income will stop unless you have money or assets set aside to replace it. Our time is also limited which puts even more pressure on making sure we are prepared for the future.

What is your wealth potential? Your wealth potential is a concept that looks at the money you will earn from the perspective of its maximum potential value. Suppose you could save and invest every dollar you ever earned. Of course, this is not possible, but understanding this concept may help you look at your money in a different light.

Opportunity cost is an economic term which assumes that every dollar has a greater potential value than the dollar itself. If you lose a dollar that you did not have to lose, you not only lost the dollar, but you also lost what it could have earned had you been able to keep it. You have two choices with every dollar you earn. You can spend it or save and invest it. If you could earn 5% on your dollar and you chose to save and invest it, your dollar could be worth a dollar plus 5%. When you spend a dollar, it is costing you a dollar plus the 5% you could have had if you had invested it. When you buy something, do you consider the cost of what those dollars could have earned? If you consider the cost of the tax you had to pay to have a dollar, the value of a dollar becomes even more meaningful. Don't forget that every dollar you have to spend has first gone through the Tax Filter. The government has already reduced the value of your dollar by the amount of tax you had to pay. The fact that you have less should help you better understand the economic value of every after tax dollar.

Wealth and Income Potential

Current Age	30
Retirement Age	65
Current Income	$50,000
Income Growth	3.00
Current Savings	$0
Investment Return	5.00%

At your retirement age of 65, your income potential will be $3,023,104 and your wealth potential will be $7,093,151.

WIP: 1/2 © MoneyTrax, Inc.

If we assume someone who is 30 making $50,000 a year with an increase in income of 3% each year, their Income Potential would be just over $3,000,000 during their working years. Their wealth potential would be over $6,000,000, assuming their opportunity cost is 6%, meaning they can earn 6% on the dollars they save and invest. Obviously, we can't save everything we make; however, this does drive home the point that every dollar is valuable and only those dollars you save and invest have the potential to return more than the dollar. Every dollar that is not saved and invested reduces your wealth potential by what you spent and the interest it could have earned.

So if you follow the graph on the following page, this person makes $100,000 a year and they are age 42. Assuming a 3% inflation rate, their Income Potential will be just over $3,200,000 and their wealth potential over $6,500,000. If your tax bracket was 30%, you would have paid $973,587 in taxes until age 65; however, if there were no such thing as taxes and you could have invested those same dollars in your account, you would have been able to accumulate just under $2,000,000.

Wealth Potential vs. Expenditures

Income Allocation	
Taxes	30.00%
Debt Svc.	0.00%
Lifestyle	70.00%
Savings	0.00%

Initial Assumptions	
Current Age	42
Retirement Age	65
Current Income	$100,000
Income Growth	3.00%
Cur. Savings	$0
Rate of Return	6.00%

Taxes
Actual Paid: $973,587
Wealth Transfer: $1,956,933

Savings: $0   Spent: $6,523,110   Documentation

WIP: 2/2 © MoneyTrax, Inc.

If you spent every dollar you earned, you would have spent $2,271,702 with a wealth potential of $4,566,177. If you are following along, then you understand that you are not going to have any future if you spend everything.

Wealth Potential vs. Expenditures

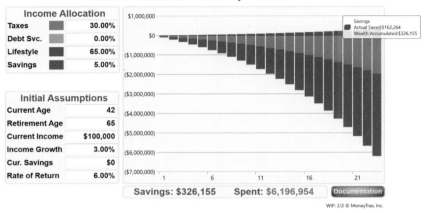

Income Allocation		
Taxes		30.00%
Debt Svc.		0.00%
Lifestyle		65.00%
Savings		5.00%

Initial Assumptions	
Current Age	42
Retirement Age	65
Current Income	$100,000
Income Growth	3.00%
Cur. Savings	$0
Rate of Return	6.00%

Savings: $326,155   Spent: $6,196,954   Documentation

WIP: 2/2 © MoneyTrax, Inc.

If you are saving 5% of your income or $5,000, which is well above the national average, you will have saved $162,264 and at 6%, your retirement account would be approximately $326,155. As you can quickly see, this probably does not look like what you had in mind for your future. We are going to give you more direction when you get to the Lifestyle Regulator on what it will take to get you where you want to be and what it will take to get you there.

Keep in mind, as we continue, there are only two ways to improve your future financial picture. The first is to focus your attention on finding investment opportunities that potentially pay higher returns, but often require more risk. The second is to be more efficient. The focus of this book is to help you find dollars you could be losing unknowingly unnecessarily and help bring those dollars back to you allowing you to put away more for your future while seeking not to impact your present standard of living.

Chapter 3: Monthly Cash Flow

nfortunately, our lifetime income potential does not come to us in a
lump sum. No matter how you get paid, most of us manage our finances
monthly. Since most of our major capital purchases such as our house
note and car loans are paid monthly, we tend to think about our money from
a monthly perspective. Access to capital plays an important role in helping us
determine our standard of living and a steady income from our employment
reduces the financial pressure required to live the lifestyle we desire.

Anything that interrupts our regular monthly cash flow creates financial
pressure everywhere else in the model. If the money you have coming in is
interrupted or reduced, it can cause major problems. If you are forced to
withdraw money from your Savings and Investment Tanks, it can cause stress
knowing you are getting behind in putting away enough for your future.
Again, in essence, you are robbing from your future lifestyle for a current
lifestyle expense. It is important to remember that your Personal Economic
Model is a pressurized system that requires steady cash flow to keep things
running smoothly and efficiently and if there is no room for the unexpected,
you will experience financial pressure.

With a solid understanding of the PEM, you should be able to better plan
your finances to remove financial pressure from your life altogether. Stress-
free living is a financial position to be desired. A good financial plan not only
considers requirements for your future, but also eliminates financial stress
today caused by the lack of access to capital. As you focus on your financial
future, make sure that you are also enjoying the journey along the way.

Setting a budget based on the flow you have coming in can save you grief
down the road from insufficient cash flow. Simply knowing what you have
coming in versus what you must pay out is prudent, but is not enough to

keep you out of financial trouble unless there is room in the budget for those unexpected expenses that will certainly come your way.

With little or no money in the Savings and Investment Tanks, it is almost certain that you are setting yourself up for financial trouble down the road. We will talk about those two tanks further later and how to utilize your money in these tanks to cover the unexpected without having to drain the tanks to solve your cash flow burdens.

While most of us do fairly well managing our monthly cash flow to cover our known fixed expenses listed in a budget, the real financial problems pop up from miscellaneous unexpected expenses that come along that must be paid. Examples may include tires for the car, a new hot water heater, braces for the kids, school supplies—the list is endless. It is the miscellaneous and unexpected expenses that come almost every month that must be managed as well if you are going to stay on top of your finances. We call these expenses major capital purchases. They are anything that you can't afford to pay for in full with monthly cash flow. This is an area where many are caught in the credit card trap because their monthly budget requires 100% of their monthly cash flow with little or no room for the unexpected. Let's face it; everything about life is unexpected.

If you are not tracking your monthly spending, you should. There are many software applications that can help you with this such as Quick Books. We recommend you find some way to track every dollar you spend. In many ways, you are like a business. Every business must account for each dollar spent and set aside dollars when times are good to cover things coming down the road. You need to track your fixed monthly expenses and record your miscellaneous expenses each month. This will give you a way to monitor your fixed and unexpected expenses, giving you a more accurate picture of the cash flow required to support the lifestyle you desire. It is quite common for our miscellaneous expenses to put such stress on our finances and without additional access to capital, this stress can cause one to make financial mistakes from which they may not recover. When you are under financial pressure, it is difficult to think as clearly as when you are not.

Without access to capital, the unexpected and miscellaneous expenses that come along are often paid with credit cards, with the intention to repay in the future. Unfortunately, there will most likely be additional miscellaneous expenses yet to come that are also going to require immediate payment, putting even greater pressure on cash flow. It does not make sense to live your financial life as if it will never rain and storms will never come. If you find yourself spending everything you make each month with nothing left over and nothing to put away for your future, it is a good sign your model is out of balance.

A budget will give you the information you need to determine where the issues are and a hint about what you need to do to fix it. The first thing that pops into mind for many is to cut back which makes sense but it hard to do and not very pleasant. The first step is to know where your money is going so you can begin making a plan.

Chapter 4:
The Tax Filter

As you look at the picture of the model, you will quickly notice that the Tax Filter takes center stage of your entire financial picture. It is impossible for you to earn one dollar without it sooner or later going through the Tax Filter. The tax law says that one must pay all the taxes required and not a penny more. If you pay more tax than required, the government is grateful for your generosity but they are not going to spend time trying to help you minimize your tax liability telling you where you could have reduced your taxes.

Avoiding unnecessary taxes can have a dramatic impact on your current lifestyle and an even greater impact on your financial future. Remember the term opportunity cost. If you pay a dollar in taxes that you did not have to pay, you not only lost that dollar, but you lost what that dollar could have earned, had you been able to keep it and invest it and earn compound interest in your own account.

The Tax Filter is very sophisticated. It knows if a dollar has been through the filter or not, and if it has, it knows if it should be taxed again and at what rate it should be taxed. There are basically three types of accounts that flow through the Tax Filter. There are some accounts that you can put your money in that can avoid going through the tax filter until you spend it during your retirement, called qualified plans. There are other accounts that require you to put in after tax dollars that grow tax deferred and the growth is taxable when you spend it called non-qualified accounts. The third type is accounts that allow contributions with after tax dollars to grow tax deferred and the money to come out tax free.

You do not have to be an expert in tax, but you do need to understand these fundamental tax positions before you can determine which accounts will work best for you in which to put your money. When talking with an advisor about any saving or investment account, you should fully understand how that account will be taxed. It is very easy to get caught up in the discussion on return and forget to discuss how that particular product will perform when the money goes through the Tax Filter.

In addition to understanding how the Tax Filter works, it would be wise to have a general understanding of the history of taxes. The federal government regulates taxes in order to be able to run the country and the amount of taxes we pay is determined by the monetary needs of the government to provide the goods and services promised. Remember that the government does not make anything, it takes what it needs. The greater its propensity to spend, the more it takes to satisfy their desire. When we have a shortage, you and I must reduce our spending and cut back. When the government needs money they get it from us, the taxpayers. This should be a concern and demand your attention since the federal government controls the income tax rates and is a partner with those who have money invested in both qualified and non-qualified accounts alike. If your account is earning interest their share is earning interest as well.

> **When we have a shortage, you and I must reduce our spending and cut back. When the government needs money they get it from us, the taxpayers.**

There was a time when America paid its expenses, especially the most expensive: wars. Unfortunately, that has not been true in recent years. Like many Americans, our government has put their expenditures on credit, paying the minimum required to get by and is in debt, paying more and more interest each year on the amount borrowed. At the writing of this book, that debt is near the twenty trillion dollar mark. Uncontrolled spending is an unsustainable practice for both the government and you as well. You will notice in the following graph of the history of taxes that if you have $300,000 in your qualified account and you are in a 30% tax bracket when you take the money your share would be approximately $210,000 and the governments share $90,000. Remember if the government needs more money they simply increase taxes to get what they need. Pay attention to the average since Congress began taking taxes in 1913. They also said at that time that taxes would be temporary. They have not missed a single year since they began.

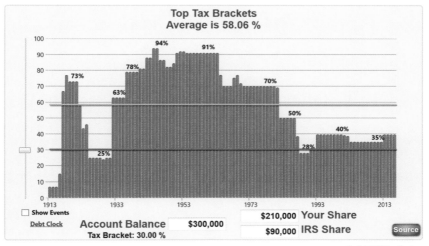

Tax Hist: 1/1 © MoneyTrax, Inc.

Chapter 5:
Qualified Plans

O ne way to get money into the Investment Tank is through qualified plans contributions.. These are retirement accounts that are "qualified," meaning the federal government has approved these accounts allowing you to make before tax contributions which allow your money to grow without being taxed until withdrawn after age 59 ½ without a 10 % penalty. You must take the required minimum distribution (RMD) beginning at age 70 ½ or incur a 50% penalty on the amount you were required to take. All withdrawals must then pass through the tax filter to be taxed as ordinary income. Some examples of such accounts you would be familiar are 401K, IRA, SEP plans, and 403b, just to name a few.

What is the major benefit of contributing to a qualified plan? Many respond saying they save taxes. It is true that you do not have to pay the taxes on the dollars you put in these plans today but you are actually postponing the taxes due until later, not saving taxes. It would be possible to save taxes if you can take your money out at a lower tax rate than you put the money in, but that may be difficult to do, especially if your plan is to enjoy an income greater than you had when you were working. You will not know if you saved taxes or not until the end when you take your withdrawals. These accounts are not tax savings accounts, but rather, tax deferred savings accounts. They simply defer the tax calculation on those dollars that you direct to an account that will be taxed in the future. We like a different word for defer: it's postpone. The government did not say you do not have to pay the tax; they said you can postpone the tax until later.

There are few qualified plan retirement options that allow you to put away aftertax dollars and have your money grow until your retirement and withdraw your money from the account tax free. These are called Roth accounts such as Roth IRA and Roth 401(k).

You have two options in these types of deferred savings accounts. One option is to pay no taxes on your contributions today and defer the taxes until you take withdrawals and the other option is to pay your taxes today and have no taxes due on withdrawals. We will look at qualified plans in greater detail later in the book when we cover the five major wealth transfers.

Not having your money in the right account could cause you to lose money unnecessarily. If you think you will pay less taxes in the future than you pay today, then postponing would be the preferred option. If you are planning on living the same or better in the future than you do today perhaps paying your taxes due up front would be best. We will provide information later that can help with this decision.

Chapter 6:
The Lifestyle Regulator

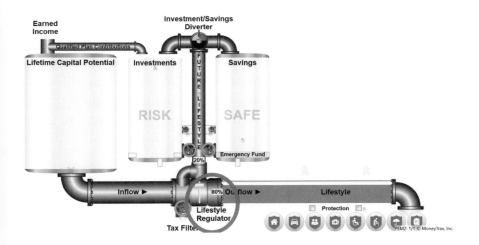

The most important piece of your Personal Economic Model is the Lifestyle Regulator. Its function is to help you see where you are today in relation to your future and help you find a balance between your current lifestyle desires and your future lifestyle requirements. You alone control the flow of money through the lifestyle regulator. If you set the valve at 100% to wide open, every after tax dollar flows directly to your current lifestyle to support your standard of living. If you set the regulator to 90%, then the regulator will push 10% up through the Future Lifestyle Tube into your Savings or Investment Tanks and allow the remaining 90% to flow to your current lifestyle to be consumed.

Your financial future depends solely on what you pump into the Savings and Investment Tanks. It is easy to see in the picture of the model that with little or nothing in the tanks, your financial future will be bleak and the journey along the way may not be a very pleasant one either. Unfortunately, in the beginning, it is easy to focus your financial attentions on how you live today, ignoring the fact that you are also responsible for your future lifestyle as well. The Lifestyle Regulator will provide answers to the four toughest financial questions we all face about our retirement and that information will give you direction in helping to determine what you will need to do to make sure you can live in the future like you live today and have your money last until your life expectancy.

The four questions are:

1: Do you know what rate of return you need to earn on the money you have today to be able to live in the future like you live today, adjusted for inflation, without running out of money before your life expectancy?

2: Do you know how much you need to be saving on a monthly or annual basis to make sure you will have enough in the future for you to live like you live today adjusted for inflation?

3: Do you know how long you will have to work doing what you are doing now before you will be able to live on what you have accumulated and your money last to your life expectancy?

4: Do you know how much you will have to reduce your standard of living during retirement the future to keep your money from running out before your life expectancy?

If you do not know the answers to these questions, it is almost impossible to know if what you are doing is going to get you to where you what to be. Knowing the answers to these questions is just the beginning. The real work begins by tackling the things you will have to do to bring your current lifestyle and your future lifestyle into balance.

There is a good chance that when you put your numbers in the Lifestyle Regulator calculator you may find you may be behind in your savings for your future. You may already know you are not doing enough for your future, but the demands of today are so great, you may feel you can't worry about your future right now. One of the reasons people avoid this conversation is they believe that the only way to find balance is to give up something. While that may be necessary for some, simply being more efficient can make a huge difference and free up dollars previously being lost to help you achieve balance.

If you find your finances out of balance you basically have three options. The first is to cut back by reducing your present standard of living which is not very exciting. The second is to take more risk with the dollars you are saving today to hopefully make up for the shortfall with a better rate of return. This option while possible does not work out often. The third option is to begin looking at opportunities to be more efficient by uncovering areas where you could be losing money unknowingly and unnecessarily. Unknowingly means you are forgiven. Unnecessarily means you can fix it.

To bring your finances into balance it may require you to do some of all three of the options we just discussed however we believe it makes sense to begin with looking for opportunities to solve the problem first by focusing on eliminating the inefficiencies. Our philosophy again is we believe there is more opportunity to increase your wealth by avoiding the losses than picking the winners.

There is a myth that if you are young, you have plenty of time to worry about such things. The truth is that the sooner you get started, the better off you will be. Another myth promoted by the financial world, especially to our youth, is that you should take investment risk early because you have time to recover from loss. The truth is that you cannot afford to lose, ever. When you lose money, you will never get that money back again. Don't forget the economic term called opportunity cost. If you lose a dollar, you not only lost the dollar, but you lost what it could have earned for you had you not lost it. You may be fortunate enough to get back to where you were before the loss, but that is not winning.

We are not talking just about the dollars you may lose from poor investment decisions which you are putting away for your future lifestyle but also the rest of the dollars you are spending to support your current lifestyle. It is here that the biggest potential for loss occurs. More dollars will go through your hands to fund your current lifestyle than you are putting away for your future. We will discuss the five major areas of wealth transfers in detail in the second half of the book, so that you can see where you might be able to find money without reducing your lifestyle today.

Financial mistakes of our past can often push one to take even more risk trying to overcome the shortfall created by unnecessary losses early. Greater knowledge about how money works, the products you choose to put your money, and how you can be more efficient are keys to your future success. We are constantly being bombarded by advertising saying this product or investment is the key to your financial success. You will have to buy financial products to secure your future but the process is more important than the product.

Let me tell you a little story to help you better understand what I am saying. Suppose I were to send you to play in the Masters, golf's most prestigious event. I have two things to give you—you can only choose one. You can have the clubs of anyone that has ever played a round of golf or you can have their ability. Which would you choose? Of course, you would choose the ability. The "swing" is much more valuable than the "club."

What is it that the financial institutions deliver? They have products which we are going to call the "clubs." It is true that you want the finest clubs made and custom fit if you are going to perform at your maximum potential, but it makes more sense to focus first on mastering the swing and by that we mean avoiding potential and unnecessary losses before fitting you for the clubs.

In the game of golf there are a few great shots in every round and on occasion the tournament is won with the greatest shot ever witnessed but that does not happen often. Tournaments are most often lost from poor shots. Shots hit out of bounds, in the woods or in the water. These shots impose a penalty in addition to the poor execution. The same is true with our finances. If your financial future depends on you hitting a perfect shot under pressure to win the odds are not in your favor.

If you stop and think about it most sporting events are not won on great plays, although we like to watch those highlights. Most are lost on mistakes. In football, it's fumbles or dropped passes that should have been caught. In baseball, it is errors or poor base running. No matter what sport you think of, it's the mistakes that keep us from the winners' circle.

Make sure your financial strategy is focusing not only on where you can put your money to earn the best returns, but that your strategy is first as efficient as it can be. Your success depends less on the "club," and more on the "swing."

The four areas addressed by the Lifestyle Regulator again are:

What rate of return do you need to earn?

How much do you need to be saving?

How long will you have to work before you will have enough to live off of what you have accumulated?

How much you will have to reduce your present standard of living if you do not do something different?

You will be pleasantly surprised to learn that in the final chapters of this book, you may be able to find enough dollars you are currently losing to bring your finances into balance without you having to change how you live today. We will be covering five areas where you should focus your attentions to make sure you are as efficient as possible before you look for the perfect investment opportunity that will solve all your financial problems with return. The answer will most likely be found by managing the information you learn from the Lifestyle Regulator to give you the best possible outcome for your future based on where you are financially today. The solution will not be found in the "clubs," but in the "swing." The answer is not in the products but the process. In golf, your chances for success are greatly improved, if you can stay out of trouble and avoid the penalties. Good luck at the Masters.

Chapter 7:
Current Lifestyle

The natural flow for our money is through Monthly Cash Flow Tube—through the Tax Filter, through the Lifestyle Regulator, and on to our current lifestyle. Perhaps the most striking thing about the Current Lifestyle Tube is the fact that all the money that gets in this tube is spent and gone forever, with the one exception of the money you pay for your house. It is important that you understand that your house is a current lifestyle expense and not an investment.

When you pay extra on your mortgage loan, does the value of your house go up?

Do your payments go down?

Can you easily get to the money without having to pay to do it?

The money in your house does not earn interest or compound interest. The value of the house either appreciates or depreciates. When you consider all the expenses involved in owning a house, it becomes very hard to think of it being an investment and if you still want to call it an investment, it may very well be the worst investment you have ever made.

Later in Chapter 15 we will have this conversation in depth and illustrate that your house is a great place to sleep and raise a family but it is not a great investment and has the potential to be your largest wealth transfer other than taxes.

There are two major capital purchases that you must make that will have the greatest impact on your monthly cash flow. The first is where you will live. Whether you pay rent or pay a mortgage payment, this will usually be one of your largest expenses. The second is your transportation, such as monthly car payments.

Your housing expense and transportation costs along with taxes account for your largest cash outlay. Involved in your decision of where you will live and what cars you will drive is the fact that you must also have money to cover other lifestyle expenses such as food, clothing, entertainment, and vacations; not to mention the money it will take for you to save and invest for your future. Already this is getting to be quite a juggling act to manage.

In addition to those things just mentioned, you must factor in the amount of cash flow required to cover the cost of the protection products that are necessary to make sure you can continue to enjoy the standard of living you have today and protect your future lifestyle. Those expenses are: auto, home, medical, disability, term life, and umbrella or liability insurance. If something or someone can take what you have accumulated, it is not really yours so it must be protected against potential loss. Protection products play a vital role in both the ability for you to maintain your present lifestyle and the lifestyle you hope to enjoy in the future.

The best way I can explain it to you is that there is a constant battle going on in your financial life between your current lifestyle desires and your future lifestyle requirements. Which side would you say is winning at your house? The hard thing about this battle is you are the general in charge on both sides. You must design a plan so that both sides win and it will not be easy.

If you are like many Americans, you would have to agree that your current lifestyle is getting the most attention. Perhaps you think you are doing pretty well or maybe you feel that your future lifestyle is getting massacred. The purpose of this book is to provide insight into how money works and sound financial concepts and information to help you to determine where you are today, and what you can do to get in the financial position you desire. Time puts even more stress on the situation because the clock is ticking when we will not be able to work any longer or life is cut short.

It is interesting that many people spend more time planning their annual vacation or cutting their grass than they spend planning their financial future. No one said it would be easy to find balance between what you want today and what you will need tomorrow, but it is doable if you understand how things work and you have a plan. The Personal Economic Model is designed to assist you in seeing what you need to do to make financial freedom possible. Remember that it will not be found in a financial product (club) but rather the process (the swing).

Let me say one last thing about current lifestyle. Remember when we looked at your lifetime capital potential? We looked first at your income potential which showed the amount of money you will earn over your lifetime which was a large number. Then we calculated your wealth potential assuming you could invest every dollar you earn. You can't do that, but you need to understand that every dollar you spend in current lifestyle has a cost greater than the dollar spent. You must also calculate what that dollar could have been worth had you kept it and put it in your Savings or Investment Tank.

If you are going to manage your current lifestyle, you need to look at the dollars you spend on those items, understanding what they really cost. Every dollar spent today is taking away from the potential you have to save and invest those dollars for your future. You have two choices with every dollar you receive. One choice is to save and invest it and the other choice is to spend it. Keep in mind the dollars you spend will never return.

This is not to suggest you should not spend and enjoy the money you earn. It is just a reminder that the dollars you spend to maintain your current lifestyle will not help you with the dollars you will need to support your future lifestyle. The only thing that will help you in the future is filling your Savings and Investment Tanks.

Chapter 8:
The Investment Tank

When one has a discussion about their financial future, the first thing that comes to mind of course is the Investment Tank. This is where one would expect to find investment products that could produce the greatest potential for the highest returns. Another word almost synonymous with investments is risk. You will notice that when you look closely at the PEM, the Investment Tank does not have a cap. This is to signify the fact that money in this tank can evaporate, meaning there is always a risk that you could lose some, part, or even all of your money, depending on the underlying account. Obviously there are ways to help minimize one's risk in this tank, but risk should always be a concern.

Our purpose in this conversation is not to give advice on where you should invest your money in specific investment products or accounts, but to give you a basic understanding of what you would expect to find in this tank. In a brief overview of types of accounts one would find in this tank, at the top of the list would be stocks, bonds, mutual funds, real estate and if you own a company, your business. There are almost as many different individual products available to the consumer as there are hairs on your head. There are no bad financial products, just as there are no bad "clubs" in a golf bag. Different products are designed to accomplish different things and at times, every product could be the best "club" to have in your hand and at other times, they could be the worst.

To continue with our golf analogy, the driver is the club that is designed to hit the ball the farthest. Money contributed to the Investment Tank is done with the expectation that it will render the potential for return on the investment. In golf, the driver is the club designed to hit the ball a long way but it is also the club that brings with it the highest risk of hitting the ball into trouble, in the water or even out of bounds. There are clubs that hit the ball shorter distances that bring confidence when the shot demands you to be precise. Then there is the putter. There is almost no risk that you could lose your ball with a putter in your hands. Distance would never be mentioned in a discussion about putters and every professional golfer would say that the putter is the most valuable club in the bag.

You must have money in both tanks. You will need accounts that provide the opportunity for gain and you also need money in accounts where you cannot lose. You will need both a driver and a putter in your financial bag to play successfully.

You will find both qualified and non-qualified investment accounts in the Investment Tank. Qualified means that the account that holds your money is "qualified" by the federal government to receive contributions before being taxed, grow tax deferred, and taxed later at the time of withdrawal.

Non-qualified accounts are those that are purchased with aftertax dollars. There are products that allow the money in these accounts to grow tax deferred meaning the growth will not be taxed until you access the money. There are accounts where the gain is taxed annually at ordinary or capital gains rates. Money deposited in these accounts are not taxed because those dollars have already gone through the tax filter and taxed when earned.

Though we are not going to talk about any individual investments inside this tank, there is a discussion you need to understand when it comes to rate of return. The Investment Tank is all about rate of return and appreciation. You should understand there is a difference between average and actual returns. The money in this tank does not compound interest uninterrupted but rather, it appreciates or depreciates and non-qualified accounts are interrupted by taxes levied on the gain.

I had a good friend named Norman Baker from Texas who used to explain dollar cost averaging like this: If your left foot is in a bucket of ice water and your right foot is in a bucket of boiling water, on average, you are doing fine.

Let me explain this with a mathematical illustration. Suppose I could guarantee you an average return of 25% over the next four years; would you want to invest in that opportunity? Most offered this opportunity in the investment world would jump at the chance.

So to participate, you must invest $100,000 on day one. Over the course of the first year, let's say you earn a 100% return moving your account balance to $200,000 by year two. You are a happy camper. During year two, the market drops and you have a negative return of 50%. Year three, you are back on track with a 100% return but in year four, you take another 50% loss. Your account balance at the end of the 4th year is $100,000, which is the same amount you started with and your average return during those four years as promised was 25% with an actual return of 0%.

When looking at any investment opportunity, remember that there is a difference between average and actual returns illustrated and do not forget to weigh the impact of the tax liability on interest earned.

Average Return vs. Actual Return

Initial Balance			$100,000
Year	Annual Return	Annual Gain/(Loss)	End of Year Account Balance
1	100.00%	$100,000	$200,000
2	-50.00%	$-100,000	$100,000
3	100.00%	$100,000	$200,000
4	-50.00%	$-100,000	$100,000
	0.00%		

Average Return: 25.00 %   **Actual Return: 0.00 %**

Chapter 9:
The Safe Tank

You will notice that the Safe Tank has a cap, meaning the dollars deposited into this tank cannot be lost. This is the fundamental difference between the Safe Tank and the Investment Tank. People putting money into this tank are more concerned about safety and a modest return than growth. Everyone who is putting money in the Investment Tank should also have a good stash of cash in the Safe Tank as well.

In our golf analogy, the "putter" would certainly be a "club" you would find in this account. Some common accounts you would see in this tank would be checking and savings accounts, certificates of deposit, money market accounts, and cash value life insurance.

> **Some common accounts you would see in this tank would be checking and savings accounts, certificates of deposit, money market accounts, and cash value life insurance.**

Money placed in these types of accounts must first pass through the Tax Filter. Once taxed, the basis or the amount of the original deposit will not be taxed in the future; however, any gain will be subject to tax each and every year you show a profit. The one exception is a permanent life insurance policy. Permanent means the contract provides for the accumulation of cash value in addition to the death benefit. The death benefit from a life insurance policy comes to the beneficiary tax free. Permanent insurance resides in the Safe Tank, not the Investment Tank. While the names given to some of these contracts may sound like an investment opportunity they are not. By law permanent life insurance can't be called an investment.

The contribution to the policy is paid with aftertax dollars and the interest earned in the policy is tax deferred during the accumulation period and at death, the proceeds are received by the beneficiary, tax free. There are also opportunities for access to the cash value in the form of tax-free loans during the accumulation period which provide the benefit of access to capital along with other benefits as well. We will cover this topic in detail in Chapter 22 because of the tremendous level of misunderstanding surrounding this product.

The commonality of all of the accounts found in the Safe Tank is that the underlying cash is easily accessible.

Chapter 10:
The Diverter Valve

Once you have determined how much you should be pumping up the Future Lifestyle Tube, the Diverter Valve will help you determine how you should divide your dollars between the Safe and Investment Tanks. Keep in mind that over your lifetime, you should expect the percentages to change. Common wisdom would suggest that the younger you are, the more you should have in the Investment Tank during your accumulation years and as you grow older, you will lean more to having more in the Safe Tank during your distribution years.

Unfortunately, common wisdom is not always the best. Many people start their savings and investment journey with 100% of their future lifestyle cash flow going into the Investment Tank and nothing in the Safe Tank. We talked earlier about those that put their money in their qualified plans (401(k), IRA, SEP, 403b), chasing return with no access to those dollars until their retirement age. It is interesting but there is rarely a good time to access capital from assets in the Investment Tank. If you are earning a high rate of return, it makes little sense to withdraw money to make a current lifestyle expense if you could finance the purchase at a lower interest rate and allow your money to keep growing at the higher return rate. If the market is down, it is not a great time to take withdrawals from the investment account because it reduces the amount in the account earning interest and you need to leave it in the account if you expect the market to rebound.

Having money in an account that you cannot access can create a great deal of stress when something comes along and you must have money. It is an easy temptation to reach for your credit card to pay for the expense and you can get caught in the trap of paying more interest to the credit card company than you are earning in your investment account.

Think of it like our discussion earlier of a boat heading upstream against the current. If your money is earning more interest than you are paying, you are still moving forward. If you are paying more interest than you are earning, you are going backwards. If the interest rate you are earning is the same as you are paying, you are just treading water.

Advisors have common recommendations on asset allocation models and diversification recommendations that can help you determine how much you should consider putting into each tank depending on your age, current assets, and current income. You can get those off the internet, but let's look at three things you should consider that can help you determine the amount you think would be good for you to split between your Investment and Savings Tanks.

Those three things are: Risk, Taxation, and Accessibility

Risk: When you think about risk ask yourself this question. Just how much money are you willing to lose? We all want the highest return possible but no one likes to lose. If I were to ask you what rate of return would you like to achieve, you may say the highest possible but keep in mind that although some investment opportunities offer the potential for bigger returns, they also come with bigger potential for loss. Risk and reward are a lot like a teeter-totter. Trying to earn the highest rate of return can also expose you to a bigger potential loss. Our philosophy is that there is more to be had in avoiding the losses in life than picking the winners. You have a philosophy today. Look at what you are doing with your money and you will be able to determine what you believe. Are you a spender or a saver? Do you save first then spend or do you spend first then save what's left over? Do you live by your philosophy or does how you live explain your philosophy? Your philosophy is something that will change over time as you gain experience. Experience can best be described by things you learned that you would not do again if you could do things over. Experience is not always the best teacher but what you learn is costly.

Let's assume you are going to save 20% of your annual income and that amount is $20,000. How much do you feel you would want to put in the Investment Tank and how much in the Safe Tank? Some would say 90%-10%, others might say 70-30, some may say 50-50, and some, 10-90.

This is more of a personal decision and as I said, it will change over time

Given a choice would you want more or less risk? Most of us would probably say we are risk adverse meaning given the same outcome we would choose less risk rather than more.

Another question would be are you more interested in what your future could be like or what it will be like?

For those who have money invested already, I think the most important thing is to make sure that the risk you are willing to take is the amount of risk you are actually taking. Times change and you should constantly review your risk position. During a lifetime of investing, some of your investments will pay off and some will not. I have a wise friend who once told me that no deal is ever as good as it was promised to be or as bad as it could be. Make sure that where you are in your investments is the place you want to be.

Taxation: One of the first things you should consider on where you should put your money is the tax ramifications of the contribution, accumulation, and distribution of the account. Remember that if you pay a tax that you did not have to pay or could have avoided, you not only lost those dollars but what they could have earned for you had you been able to keep them.

Let me give you an example. Should you put your money in a traditional IRA or a Roth IRA? The traditional IRA will allow you to deduct the contribution from your current income reducing your current tax liability but the money will come out taxable. At what tax rate you ask? Now that is a great question. If you put it in at a lower tax rate and take it out at a higher rate, you lose. If you take it out at a lower tax rate than you put it in, you win.

The Roth IRA allows you to put the money in with after tax dollars, meaning the dollars you contribute to the account have already gone through the Tax Filter. Your money then grows tax deferred and comes out tax free. This type of account would make more sense for those who believe they will be in a higher tax bracket in the future than they are in today. The point to understand here is you need to make an intelligent decision about where you will be in the future compared to your tax rate today to make the wisest choice.

You may be asking how can I know what tax rate I will be in when I retire? Well it may not be as hard as you think. If you are not a saver, it is most probable that you will be in a lower tax bracket when you retire than you were in when working. Once your earned income from employment stops, your income in the future will depend on what you have in your tanks. No money in the tanks will usually mean less income. You will most likely have less than you would need to allow you to continue at your working income level, putting you in a lower tax bracket.

If you are one who has managed to balance their current lifestyle desires with their future lifestyle requirements, your goal would be to have enough to live like you live today adjusted for inflation through your life expectancy. To do that, you are going to need to be a saver. How much you need to save will depend on when you get started.

If the lion share of your money is in qualified accounts and you have not been a good saver, it would be reasonable to think you could be in a lower bracket since you will need to reduce your withdrawals to avoid running out of money before your life expectancy. With insufficient dollars in your account should you continue spending the same amount as you did when working, your account would deplete before your life expectancy. Remember that every dollar that comes out of your qualified account must then pass through the Tax Filter and will be taxed as ordinary income.

Don't forget the government does not make money; they appropriate or take what they need. They can't take money from those who have none; so where else are they going to go but to those that have it? Don't forget you have a partner if you have money in a qualified plan and your partner will decide the rate at which they want their share. The government has always taxed the rich and this trend will only increase when you consider the amount of government promises that have been made to those who did not save or invest the money they earned.

When a famous bank robber, Willy Sutton, was caught, he was asked why he robbed banks. He said because that is where they keep the money. Where is the money today, and who has the keys? To find out more about who the government believes is rich look closer at the Tax Filter in chapter 16.

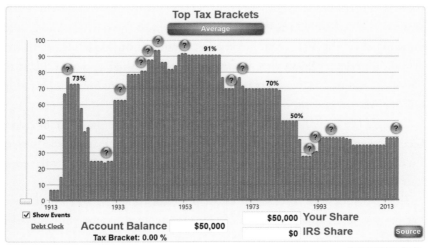

Tax Hist: 1/1 © MoneyTrax, Inc.

Accessibility: This decision I believe is even more important than the first two mentioned but is often ignored. Planning for your future is important and the lack of planning can cause a great deal of stress in your later years if you are not prepared. No access or insufficient access to capital can cause unbelievable stress in your current lifestyle and impact your income potential because your Personal Economic Model is under pressure. It is unfortunate but many Americans live under crushing financial pressure their entire life that could be reduced or eliminated if they understood the power of access to capital. Many have money but it is tied up in accounts that they can't get their hands on to help them over the unexpected expenses that life brings our way. They can't get to the dollars in their 401(k) because they are not age 59 ½ or more. They have money in their house but the housing market values may be down. They have money in real estate but would have to sell.

If your income is reduced, it creates pressure because of your current lifestyle obligations which you must keep your promise to pay or you could lose everything. Money lost in the market creates stress and pressure trying to get back to where you were before the loss. Going to work every day knowing that there are not enough hours in the day for you to earn enough money to cover your current expenses much less be prepared for retirement is depressing.

There is tremendous stress as you grow older knowing that you have not done enough to be where you need to be financially and the day is coming when you will not be able to earn an income any longer. Using a credit card to cover current lifestyle expenses without being able to pay the balance in full at the end of the month creates stress because you know you are on a slippery slope and one step away from financial ruin.

Living a life free of financial stress can be worth more than rate of return. Access to capital is the only remedy to eliminate financial stress. Focusing on the critical balance between your Investment and Savings Tanks will reduce your stress and allow you to enjoy the journey along the way.

This concludes our discussion on the pieces of the PEM and we trust that you have a better understanding of what is involved to put your model in order. Here are a few things you should walk away with from your review of the Personal Economic Model.

You will have a lot of money go through your hands during your lifetime.

You have great potential

You have a Tax Filter provided to you by the state and federal governments.

Every dollar you earn must eventually pass through the Tax Filter.

The Lifestyle Regulator regulates the flow between your Current and Future Lifestyle Tubes.

The Lifestyle Regulator provides the information to bring your model into balance.

You need to know the answers to the four toughest financial questions.

The natural flow for your money is through the Tax Filter to your current lifestyle and gone forever.

Money spent on your current lifestyle will never return to you.

The Future Lifestyle Tube goes up to suggest it takes energy and effort to pump money into the tanks.

The Investment Tank has no cap which suggests money can evaporate.

Dollars in the Investment Tank are at risk.

Your money in your 401(k) or qualified plans postpones your tax and the tax calculation.

Qualified savings accounts are not tax savings account; they are tax deferred savings accounts.

The Safe Tank has a cap signifying dollars in this tank can't be lost unless withdrawn.

Access to capital may be more important than rate of return.

Your Personal Economic Model is under pressure.

Position A is finding a balance between current lifestyle desires and future lifestyle requirements.

In the next portion of the book we will begin to provide information and strategies that will help you find the balance you desire and focus on how you can do that without having to impact your present standard of living.

Chapter 11:
The Circle of Knowledge

What you don't know may be more important than what you do know.

At this point, you should be comfortable with the model and we are ready to start talking about how to efficiently manage the flow of money into, through and out of the model.

There has probably been more written about money than any other subject on the planet and yet in the last 100 years with all the knowledge available, there has been little change in the percentage of those who have money and those who have little. I have always been puzzled by that statistic and I certainly am not saying that you will find the answer to that problem in this book, but part of the answer lies not in the financial products that we have available to us but rather, a better understanding of the process of how money works.

Isn't it interesting that we spend a small fortune on an education that will help us get a good job with a good income, but in our educational process we were taught little or nothing about what to do with the money we make or how it works? We watched our parents and family from the sidelines and how they handled money and came up with our own philosophy. They seem to be doing well; so we try to copy them without really understanding how they did it. In many homes, how to manage money is a private matter and never discussed. We also listen to the financial "experts" on television and the radio who are talking to the masses, who tell us what they think we should do and yet we still struggle financially.

The balance of this book will be more about the "swing" (process) and very little about the "clubs" (products). It seems that the experts like to talk more about "where" we should put our money before they tell us "how" we should handle our money.

Let me tell you a story we call the "Circle of Knowledge."

Circle Of Knowledge

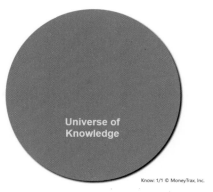

Know: 1/1 © MoneyTrax, Inc.

This circle represents all of the information in the known universe. Everything that is known that can be known.

Circle Of Knowledge

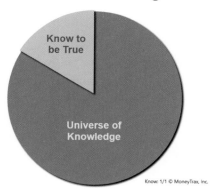

Know: 1/1 © MoneyTrax, Inc.

The top left slice of the circle represents the information that you know, and you know that you know it. Some examples are: your name, your birthdate, the names of your spouse, and your children and your social security number. You know a lot of things but in the universe of knowledge, you have to admit that what we as individuals know would barely show up on the radar. Don't feel bad because that is true for each one of us.

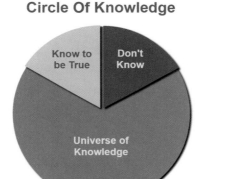

The top right slice of the circle represents that information that you know about but do not fully understand. You know these things are "out there" but you really don't know anything about them.

Some examples might be nuclear physics or how to perform brain surgery.

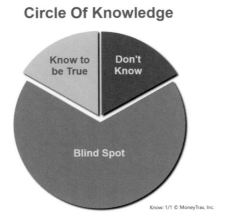

The rest of the information in the universe of knowledge represents information that you don't know, and you don't even know that you don't know it. You are unconsciously incompetent in these areas. The fact that we don't know anything about it doesn't mean that the information doesn't exist. It just means that we are currently unaware of its existence. This information is currently sitting in your "blind spot."

In this book, we are talking about finances. It is probable that the some of the information we will discuss resides in all three of the areas of knowledge we just mentioned. Some information you will already know, some you think you know, and some you may have never heard before today. Part of increasing your circle of knowledge is keeping an open mind and looking at things from a different perspective.

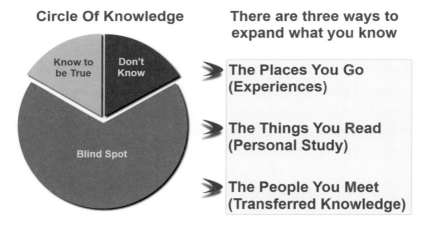

Know: 1/1 © MoneyTrax, Inc.

Our hope is to help you expand your circle of knowledge about money and acquaint you with financial truths that can help you improve your current and future financial position. There are three ways to expand what you know.

The first is the experiences you have from the places you go. You could go to a place of higher learning and study everything they can teach you about money, finance, and economics. This may not be an option because of the time constraints involved. Another problem is that once you have the personal experience, you have less time to put what you have learned into practice. "If I could go back I would do things differently" is said by many when it comes to how we would handle our money.

Another option is through personal education you get from the information you read. We do learn a great deal from our reading but what to read can be an issue. There is so much information available today that deciphering what is true and what is not true can be difficult. A good rule of thumb is that if what you read does not make sense to you, then you probably should ignore it.

The final way is through others you meet where they transfer their knowledge to us. Most of what we know has been transferred to us from someone else who is more knowledgeable about the subject than we may be and preferably an expert. We pay a doctor for their wisdom about the human body. We pay a mechanic for their knowledge of how to fix our cars

> **Most of what we know has been transferred to us from someone else who is more knowledgeable about the subject than we may be and preferably an expert.**

and get us on the road again. Our incomes are derived from others paying for information they need or want from us. We buy products we can't produce ourselves that we want or need and those people who developed those products are paid from their knowledge on how to make them.

This is where this book can be of great help to you. The good news is that there is certainly a great deal of information you already "know" about money. However, some of the ideas in this book may currently be sitting in your blind spot or may be things you know about but do not fully understand. Our desire is to offer solid financial information that is practical and understandable to increase your circle of knowledge about money and how to make your money work better for you. The more efficiently you handle your money the more you will have to spend or save.

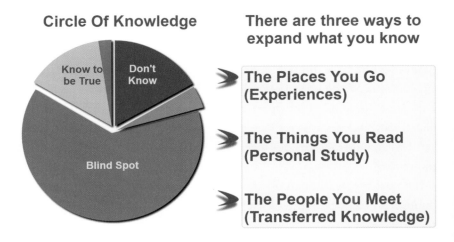

Circle Of Knowledge

Know to be True

Don't Know

Blind Spot

There are three ways to expand what you know

The Places You Go
(Experiences)

The Things You Read
(Personal Study)

The People You Meet
(Transferred Knowledge)

Know: 1/1 © MoneyTrax, Inc.

The purple slice of pie represents financial information that sits somewhere between what you know and information in your blind spot. We hope to help you take that information you learn in this book that sits in this purple slice and move it to the area of things you "know" and you "know" that you "know."

The little slice of red represents things that you know about money that may not be true but you believe to be true. You may read some things in this book that will challenge what you believe to be true. You will be left with two choices. One is to ignore the information and the other is to replace what you once thought to be true with new information that is true and you "know" that it is true.

> **You may read some things in this book that will challenge what you believe to be true. You will be left with two choices. One is to ignore the information and the other is to replace what you once thought to be true with new information that is true and you "know" that it is true.**

Let's get back to the experts. Who are the experts? The cost to be on national radio is expensive and even more expensive to be on national television. Those who use these platforms are interested in one thing, making money. Who are the radio and TV experts talking to? Is the information you hear from these venues designed for you or the masses? Who is paying these people to spread the information you are hearing and what is it that they want us to buy with that information?

Let's play a little game. Would you say you have a common income or an uncommon income? It is interesting that most who are asked that question respond with common. It is easy to look around and see how everyone else is living and think that everyone makes more money than you do. It is also easy to believe we have a common income because those we work with all have about the same standard of living we do.

Let's see if your income is common or uncommon. How much money do you think you have to earn to be in each of the percentages of household incomes in America?

The Income Game

To be in The Top	Household AGI Income Split Point	Percentage of Overall Taxes Paid	
1%	?????		
5%	?????		
10%	?????		
25%	?????		
50%	?????		

IG: 2/2 © MoneyTrax, Inc.

Go ahead and write in your answers. Start at the bottom and work your way to the top. It is important that you write in your answers before you turn the page and see the answers. Okay, turn the page.

The Income Game

To be in The Top	Household AGI Income Split Point		Percentage of Overall Taxes Paid
1%	?????	$ 465,626	
5%	?????	$ 188,996	
10%	?????	$ 133,445	
25%	?????	$ 77,714	
50%	?????	$ 38,173	

Source

IG: 2/2 © MoneyTrax, Inc.

What did you learn? If you cheated and did not write down anything, you probably learned nothing. Compare what you thought to be true with what is actually true. Unless you are a CPA, you probably missed by a mile. The point is that what we think to be true may not be true at all but what we believe can drive a false narrative of reality. We act on our perception of reality until our perception is changed by new information that we now know is true, allowing us to replace what we once believed with new more accurate truth. Now that you have new information which has been validated, would you say you have a common income or and uncommon income?

If you make more than 75% of wage earners in America, you do not have a common income if you make more than $77,000. Who are the financial experts talking to? There are 1.4 million households in the top 1% income bracket, with the average being $465,626. You can't have a TV show with that small of a potential audience. There are only 14 million in the top 10%. The average income for that group is $133,445. That is still not enough viewers to host a TV show. There are 35 million in the top 25% and that may be sufficient to have a radio show but not TV. There are 70 million in the top 50% and now you have enough for TV and radio.

The point here is that if you are talking to the masses, you have to give information that applies to the masses. If you have a common income, you will find it difficult to get uncommon information listening to those talking to folks with common incomes about what they should do with their money. Our tendency is to apply the same common ideas and strategies we learned when we had a common income to our new higher uncommon income. When our income becomes uncommon, it is often difficult to change our thinking from what we have done in the past. Unfortunately, most of the financial services industry is only looking for those with very high uncommon incomes and those with common incomes never get the information that could positively impact their financial future.

The Personal Economic Model is designed for people of all incomes. This book was written to share information that can help everyone be more efficient with their resources. Whether one has a common or uncommon income, the fundamentals are the same. Obviously one must have an income that provides enough money to cover basic living expenses and enough left over to be able to save for the future. This poses a tremendous problem for many Americans who are concerned with survival in our country.

If you have an uncommon income, you would expect uncommon knowledge that applies specifically to your financial situation. Make sure you know where your information is coming from and if it is appropriate for your level of income. Don't be afraid to challenge what you know about money to make sure it is accurate.

Chapter 12:
Protection: It's Not Yours if Someone or Something Can Take It

In keeping with the concept that there is more to be had in avoiding the losses than picking the winners, having the proper type and amount of protection in place plays an important role in making sure that your financial future is not interrupted or destroyed. Unfortunately, spending time on protection is less exciting than talking about investment opportunities but in the long run the time you spend here could prove to be the best time spent.

The purpose of this book is not to make you an expert in protection but rather to give insight into the basics of each and alert you to things that could cause you great financial harm. You are going to need to find an advisor who specializes in these areas to help you secure the proper amounts but this discussion should help you be better prepared for your conversation with that advisor. If someone or something can take what you have from you, then it's not really yours; you just have it temporarily.

When you look at the areas of protection from the model view, you should understand that none of them move you forward financially. They do not add any value to your Savings and Investment Tanks but they do provide a tremendous value to your economic model in keeping you from going backwards. There are all kinds of insurance products available that provide protection from loss. Without the proper protection in place, you would be forced to drain your savings and investment tanks or disrupt your cash flow to recover from a loss and some losses could be catastrophic sending you into financial ruin.

I have often heard people say I am insurance poor. I chuckle inside thinking they have no idea of how poor they would be if they had none. There is no doubt insurance is an expense. A good way to look at protection and the cost to have it is that although it does not move your forward, it keeps you from going backwards. Picture yourself in a boat rowing up stream. You continue to move forward as long as you keep going. Anything that happens to keep you from moving forward means you will be going back down stream which will require more energy and effort just to get back to where you once were. Protection products act as an anchor that allow you to stay where you are in the stream and continue to move forward once the issue is solved.

Perhaps the biggest reason to have it is that there are some loses we could face that, without the proper protection, could capsize the boat and destroy everything we have accomplished. When you think about the potential cost if you do not have it, the price to have it seems more than reasonable.

I encourage you to take time to spend on each of the following areas of protection and determine if you have the amount of protection you want in place. There can be a wide range of benefits between the minimum coverage and the maximum. Insurance is designed to restore you to the position you were in before the claim. The more assets one has, the greater the need to protect them. It is up to you to make sure you have the proper coverage in place. To determine what that proper coverage is will require you to find a knowledgeable "P & C," or Property and Casualty agent, who can guide you through the products that can best minimize your risk of loss.

Auto Insurance

While it might be intuitive to think of auto insurance as coverage designed to repair/replace a vehicle due to damage done to it that line of thinking only addresses a portion of what Auto Insurance is designed to do. At the writing of this book, all states (except New Hampshire) require that the owner of a vehicle carry "liability" coverage, in the event that the driver does physical damage to someone else's vehicle or bodily injury to any of the passengers. If the owner of the vehicle sustained damage to their vehicle and subsequently wants their vehicle repaired or they were liable for damaging someone else's property, they would need "collision" coverage. If the owner of the vehicle sustained damage to their vehicle by known or unknown sources (where blame could not be placed) and subsequently wants their vehicle repaired, they would need "comprehensive" coverage. In addition to these coverages, many owners include Uninsured Motorist coverage to protect themselves in case a person who fails to carry liability coverage does damage to their vehicle. Another version of this type of coverage is Underinsured Motorist coverage to protect you in case a person who fails to carry adequate liability coverage does damage to their vehicle.

Due to its mandatory nature, many consumers fail to recognize the true financial benefit of this important protection. The financial impact of failing to have adequate Auto Insurance in place can be catastrophic to both your current lifestyle and your financial future. Many consumers elect to have the state minimums of coverage required to operate a vehicle legally looking for the least expensive policy. The inherent danger in this line of thinking is that the state required minimums are typically too low to cover the bodily injury and/or property damage claims that might result from an accident. If you have money in the tanks, you want to make sure you have adequate coverage no matter what happens.

As an example, if the state required minimum is 25/50/25 and the bodily injuries or property damage exceeds these limits, the at-fault driver will be responsible for the difference in medical claims or vehicle repair. Since you do not deal with this every day, you may not remember what the three series of numbers actually mean. In the preceding example the first 25 represents $25,000 of bodily injury coverage for a single person, the 50 represents $50,000 of bodily injury coverage for all of the passengers in the vehicle, and the last 25 represents $25,000 of property damage referring to the vehicle impacted.

Imagine yourself or one of your family members were involved in an accident with a very expensive car and today, there are many on the road that cost well over $100,000. After the insurance company repairs the car, the at-fault driver would be responsible for any shortage that their policy didn't cover. Can you imagine being responsible for a $75,000 shortage on auto repair for a car that is not even yours? It happens every day and unfortunately, when you add the potential legal costs, it is easy to understand without proper coverage you may never recover.

When you think about the total picture, it is easy to see how avoiding such a loss would be greater than the return you may have earned on a great investment opportunity.

Homeowners Insurance

Homeowners Insurance typically meets the needs of the homeowner when they understand its intended purpose. It is a coverage put in place to protect those with a vested interest (i.e. homeowner, mortgage company, etc.) from the costs associated with infrequent and catastrophic incidents. That being said, Homeowners Insurance is not designed to replace a broken window or faulty water heater, although most claims filed will be honored. The risk is that too many claims can cause a policy to become non-renewed. Homeowners Insurance can be classified by the type of structure with which it is associated. There are policies designed for "standard" and "luxury" homes, as well as policies for condos or mobile homes and to protect the contents of renters. Many policies are offered with a co-insurance amount. Co-insurance is a practice where the homeowner is required to keep a certain percentage of the value of the home in force at all times. As an example, an 80% co-insurance requirement on a $500,000 home is $400,000. When the adequate amount is maintained, the coverage performs as expected.

Standard policy coverage may be limited for various reasons. Specific perils, such as war, wear and tear, and intentional destruction of covered property by the insured, are considered uninsurable. Other perils (e.g. floods, earthquakes, etc.) are excluded because the cost of coverage tends to be relatively high or because not everyone has a need for the coverage. For those policy owners who have expensive jewelry or valuable works of art, they may need specialized coverage on those items through a homeowner's policy endorsement.

Property Valuation

Property insurance policies will use one of two approaches when determining how much insurance to purchase, and when determining how much the insurer will pay in the event of a property loss. The two approaches are Actual Cash Value basis and Replacement Cost Valuation basis. Other variations like Agreed Value are used with antiques and collectibles.

Actual Cash Value

The concept of actual cash value is based on the principle of indemnity, which means that an insured should not profit from a loss but should be put into approximately the same financial position that existed before a loss. Policies written on an actual cash value basis (such as auto physical damage and personal property under many homeowners' policies) state that losses will be settled at actual cash value at the time of loss but not in an amount greater than the amount required to repair or replace the property.

In some cases, market value is used to establish the insurable value of property. The fair market value of property is the amount for which a knowledgeable seller, under no unusual pressure, would sell the property and a knowledgeable buyer, under no unusual pressure, would purchase it. The actual cash value of an auto is usually considered to be its fair market value. It is relatively easy to establish the actual cash value of any auto, because there is an active market for autos, and the price at which comparable used cars have recently sold is readily available.

Replacement Cost

When property is valued on a replacement cost basis, no deduction is made for depreciation. Replacement cost is based on replacement with materials or items of like kind and quality as that lost. For example, if a kitchen were destroyed, the value of the loss would be determined by characteristics of the old kitchen. The insurance company would pay the cost to replace an old marble counter top with a new like-kind counter top. The insured would have to assume the extra cost if he or she wanted a new granite counter top. Similarly, the insurance company would not pay to replace standard low-cost kitchen cabinets with expensive custom-made cabinets.

Again, it is important that you purchase enough coverage to replace your home and belongings should a loss occur. Personal articles coverage is often missed by many insured to cover specific things like rings and articles of value not covered under home owners. A mistake made by many is they don't increase their coverage with the increasing value of their home. For many, this is their most valuable tangible asset and should receive the proper attention when deciding on the amount of insurance coverage required.

Development of Medical Expense Coverage

Prior to the Great Depression, ill or injured persons and their families bore the cost of their own medical expenses. Blue Cross & Blue Shield organizations were the first to develop plans to provide medical expense coverage. The market grew with the introduction of HMOs (Health Maintenance Organizations) and major medical insurance. By the 1960s, the federal government became a major player in providing medical expense coverage for the elderly and the poor through the establishment of Medicare & Medicaid. The number of uninsured Americans was approximately 45 million in 2012 and is projected to decrease to about 23 million in 2023 under the implementation of the Patient Protection and Affordable Care Act (PPACA). If repealed, the number of uninsured could increase again; however, the main point is that the widespread of medical expense insurance programs has positively impacted the financial well-being of most Americans.

Major Medical Insurance

Major medical insurance is a necessity, and in today's political environment, it is required (but could change). While some people weigh the probability of getting sick against the cost of paying an insurance premium, the odds are in favor of paying the premium to purchase coverage for the average-income American. Medical insurance pays towards the cost of the service provider and the facility where the services took place. A $40,000 hip replacement could be fully covered (i.e. doctor, anesthesiologist, hospital, etc.) under some plans. Under other plans, a routine doctor's visit for a physical could cost $300 out of pocket. The lack of major medical insurance or insufficient coverage has caused many families to lose their home or file for bankruptcy protection.

Deductibles are the self-funded portion of a medical expense plan. The majority of HMO and PPO plans have deductibles that apply both in-network and out-of-network. The use of a copayment structure and coinsurance after an insured satisfies the deductible differs according to whether care is received from a network or non-network provider.

Depending on the type of medical plan, a copayment or coinsurance may apply. Copayments tend to be the patient's portion paid to network providers for the service rendered at that time, while coinsurance is the amount of the overall bill for which the patient has responsibility. For example, a plan may have a copayment of $20 for doctor visits and $100 for an emergency room visit. It is also common for such plans to have a copayment for hospitalizations—for example, a $50 or $100 flat fee per day. If an insured uses a non-network provider, the same plan may pay 80 percent of allowable charges. Allowable charges are sometimes pegged to what the plan pays network providers, rather than actual charges. As a result, the insured will be responsible for 20 percent of allowable charges as well as any provider charges in excess of allowable charges.

For those who have considerable assets, there should be no question about owning this type of insurance protection. A single medical emergency could wipe out a lifetime of savings and investment dollars in just a few days. Again the cost to have it far outweighs the potential loss if you do not.

Disability Insurance

As you look at the model, you can easily understand that a key to maintaining your present and future standard of living depends greatly on your ability to earn an income. If your income stops, everything else in the model is affected. If you have assets set aside in the Savings and Investment Tanks, you will most certainly be forced to start draining those valuable resources without this form of protection. Not every occupation qualifies for this type of protection but if you do, it should be on the top of your list.

There are basically two types of disability coverage: long term and short term.

Long Term Disability:

How much coverage you should have is a rather simple discussion. You should purchase all the coverage you can get. The amount of coverage you can have in place is limited to about 60-70% of your current income. If your personal disability policy is paid for with after tax dollars, the benefit should you receive it comes to you tax free. If you purchase an individual policy and deduct the contribution, then any benefit received would be considered taxable. The same would be true for policies you have through your employer, since those benefits are deductible to the employer but taxable to the employee.

The real decision you need to make is not how much coverage but rather, how long can you go without the money. The benefit period is determined by what is called the elimination period which is similar to a deductible. The longer the elimination period you choose, the lower the cost. Normal periods are 30, 60, 90, 180, and 365 days, as well as two years.

The amount of money you have in the two tanks can help you make your decision when choosing the elimination period. Remember that none of the dollars spent on this protection will come back to you if you are not disabled during the scheduled time period which is usually ends at age 65 or 70. The cost must be calculated not only on the premium required but what those same dollars could have earned had they been invested. Like all protection expenses, you need to weigh the cost to have the coverage against the cost of not having it at all. If you have money in your tanks, you can more easily weather the storm until the benefit is paid allowing you to choose a longer elimination period. It comes down to deciding on how long can you go without receiving the benefit.

Short Term Disability:

This coverage is meant to cover your income needs for a short period until you can return to work. It is often purchased as a benefit from your employer and the premiums withdrawn from your weekly payroll check. While many employers automatically offer long-term disability coverage, they make the short-term disability coverage optional to the employee. Short-term disability insurance is a necessity because there is a high likelihood that an individual may be disabled during their lifetime which increases the likelihood of eroding their savings. Almost every state requires that an employer provide workers' compensation insurance to their employees if they get hurt on the job; however, the likelihood of getting hurt off the job is quite significant.

Personal tasks like cleaning the gutters, gardening, playing tennis, painting, etc. can result in a disability. Often to lower the premiums, individuals will take vacation and sick leave time before they turn on their short-term disability benefits.

This coverage is meant to cover your income needs for a short period until you can return to work. It is often purchased as a benefit from your employer and the premiums withdrawn from your weekly payroll check.

Statistics show that there is a higher probability that a person will be disabled than they are to die. But we're all going to die—how is that so? The statistics really refer to, over one's lifetime, a person has a higher probability of becoming disabled than they are to die. The probability of disability decreases and the probability of death increases as the person ages. As an example, a 25 year old male has a 36% higher probability of becoming disabled than he does of dying, whereas a 45 year old male has a 25% higher probability of becoming disabled than he does of dying.

As it relates to its financial effect on the family, the disability of a breadwinner can be much more severe than death. While it is evident that income ceases in both cases, with respect to a long-term disability, family expenses usually increase due to the cost of providing care for the disabled person. The purpose of disability income insurance is to replace (partially or totally) the income of persons who are unable to work because of accident or sickness. Statistics show that about half of all employees will have a disability that lasts at least 90 days sometime during their working years, and 1 out of every 10 persons can expect to be permanently disabled before reaching age 65.

SOURCES OF COVERAGE

Disability income protection can come from several sources (e.g. Social Security system, Medicaid, employer-provided benefits, or individual policies).

Possible Sources of Disability Income Coverage
• workers' compensation programs
• state temporary disability laws
• Social Security

- employer-provided sick-leave plans
- employer-provided short-term disability income insurance plans
- employer-provided long-term disability income insurance plans
- individual disability income insurance policies

Individual Disability Income Insurance

Many individuals have a need for disability income insurance that social insurance and employer-provided benefits do not meet. Although some disability income companies do not insure persons in certain hazardous occupations, other insurers offer a special disability policy for these occupations. In the event that the employer-sponsored benefits cease or are reduced, an increased need for individual protection arises. Additionally, it is possible to change jobs and find that the new employer does not offer disability insurance which increases the need to have an individual policy. One advantage of choosing individual protection over employer-provided group protection is that the individual is not subject to termination of coverage at the whim of management. Also, individual coverage is portable and can go with the insured as they relocate or change careers. You can't deduct the premium on personally owned coverage so the benefits paid will be tax free.

One of the most important things to consider in addition to the elimination period is the definition of disability. Do you qualify for a policy that in the event you can't do your specific job you receive a benefit or do your benefits decrease if you can do any job? Pay attention to this next section.

Definition of Disability

Benefits are paid under disability income insurance contracts only if the employee meets the disability definition as specified in the contract. Virtually all short-term disability income insurance contracts define disability as the total inability of the employee to perform the duties of his regular occupation (also known as "own-occupation"). A small minority of contracts use a more restrictive definition (also known as "any-occupation"), requiring that an employee be unable to engage in any occupation for compensation which he is qualified by reason of training, education, or experience; partial disabilities are usually not covered. Regardless of the definition of disability, the majority of short-term contracts limit coverage to non-occupational disabilities because employees have workers' compensation benefits for occupational disabilities. The purpose of using a dual definition of disability, rather than an own-occupation definition of disability, is to require and encourage a disabled employee after a period of time to adjust his or her lifestyle and earn a livelihood in another occupation.

One's greatest asset, without question, is their ability to earn their income. As we saw in the beginning review of the Personal Economic Model, one's income potential over a lifetime is significant and when we calculate those dollars at interest, their wealth potential is huge. Suppose you had a machine that would produce over $5,000,000 for you over the next 30 years—would you insure it? Sure, you would. When you consider the cost to not have disability coverage in force and a disability occur, the cost seems insignificant.

In many ways, a permanent disability can be worse than death because you are around to see the impact caused from the loss of your income. You watch your family and loved ones suffer through the additional work required to provide care for you and continue paying the bills which with your condition have increased dramatically. A disability wavier can be added to both term and permanent life insurance contracts which will waive the premium in the event of a permanent disability and pay the premium as well. Life insurance policies today can also provide access to a portion of the death benefit in the event of a critical illness. Disability coverage is an area of protection that you can't afford to be without.

Term Life Insurance
When it comes to talking about term life insurance, most of us assume this is a needs discussion. This discussion is really about "wants," not "needs." There is no one wise enough to determine what one needs—since the very thought of "need" represents the least amount. A "least" analysis approach would be to assume that if one purchased the least amount of coverage and

died, that amount would be adequate to take care of all the reasons why they purchase the coverage. I don't believe that is even possible. It would be hard to find anyone who has been successful at anything who began by calculating the least they had to do to make it. Why would we apply that thinking to the value of one's life?

Life insurance should be considered a "want" product. You decide what you "want" to happen—then it can be determined how much coverage it will take to accomplish what you want. Life insurance can provide the immediate funds to guarantee that what you want to happen will happen even in the event you are not here to see it happen.

Often the amount chosen is determined by the amount of liabilities one has should death occur. Just enough to pay off a mortgage, credit card balance, or car loan. This approach can leave a huge shortfall in what it really needed in cash flow to sustain the living. Rather than simply enough money to pay off loans a more realistic approach would be to consider how much coverage would be required to produce the cash flow necessary for heirs to continue living the standard of living they enjoy today.

> **Rather than simply enough money to pay off loans a more realistic approach would be to consider how much coverage would be required to produce the cash flow necessary for heirs to continue living the standard of living they enjoy today.**

It has been said that life insurance should be considered if you care whether someone will suffer financially if you die. Term life insurance is one of the least expensive initial ways of addressing this concern. Term life insurance is very useful when the need is temporary. As an example, if you take out a loan, the bank may require a term life policy, to guarantee they will get their money back should you die before you have the loan paid off. Term life insurance is also useful when the need is permanent, but the budget does not support the cost of a permanent (i.e. whole life) insurance policy. As an example, if you want to ensure that your spouse and 2-year old twins can enjoy the equivalent of an $80,000 income should you die prematurely, it may require $1,600,000 or even more of coverage depending on the interest rate assumption to provide that level of income. The withdrawal of principal and interest could provide a greater income stream but the underlying account holding the money will deplete faster than taking interest only from the account.

The cost of term insurance would be substantially cheaper initially but keep in mind that you also need to calculate the opportunity cost of the premiums spent at interest to fully account for the cost of owning the coverage over time. Unfortunately, the cost of term insurance does not stop when you stop payment premiums because you have lost those dollars forever. Less than 1% of term insurance policies in force actually result in a benefit being paid to the policy holder.

Picture yourself on that plane that landed on the Hudson River in New York. How much coverage do you think those people would have wanted to have in force when they heard that awful news come over the speaker that the plane was going down? A "needs analysis" would not be necessary; "just give me all the coverage they will issue" would have been the response. Why does our brain seem to work more clearly in times of stress than when everything is going just fine? Life insurance is a want product.

Long Term Care (LTC) Insurance

Research shows that the majority of Americans will need some type of long term care during their lifetime. Often this results in them not being able to accomplish two or more Activities of Daily Living (ADLs)— the physical processes consisting of bathing, eating, drinking, toileting, continence, and transferring from bed-to-chair. Often we include Instrumental Activities of Daily Living (IADLs) as well, which are mental processes and consist of preparing meals, using the phone, managing money, doing the laundry, and shopping for groceries. Once this stage of life is reached, internal/external care is needed. Often family members perform these tasks, but it may become necessary to have non-family members involved when family is unavailable or non-existent. While it is sometimes customary to pay family members for their time, it is expected that payment be made when non-family members contribute to the care. When resources are plentiful, care can be too; however, when resources are scarce, care tends to also be scarce. What are our options when care needs to be extensive like a nursing home or hospice?

The average cost across the various states is over $80,000/year and can be higher depending on the level of care required. When individuals don't have the resources to cover the costs associated with long-term care issues, they should consider LTC Insurance as is a way of prepaying on the front end for care that will probably be necessary later in life. The most cost-effective time to buy LTC Insurance is in the late 40s early 50s because after that, the cost tends to be prohibitive.

This type of coverage provides protection from having to drain the tanks you have worked so hard to fill over your lifetime. Unfortunately, the spouse that is left at home most often still has the cash flow requirement necessary on top of the added expense to care for the one who needs the care. This can cause a lifetime of savings and investments to disappear rather quickly. For those who have little money set aside to cover such an expense, Long Term Care coverage can provide tremendous stress relief just knowing they have protection.

Without coverage in place when needed, you will need to look for the resources to cover the expense.

Some Ways to Pay for Long-Term Care
- personal income and assets
- family support
- Medicaid/public assistance programs
- continuing care retirement communities
- accelerated benefits in life insurance policies
- long-term care insurance

There is a great deal more to know about this type of coverage than we can discuss and there is a great deal more you should know to be prepared for such an event. Improper planning could cause you to lose a great deal or even all you have worked to achieve during your lifetime.

Liability Insurance

The final area of protection we need to discuss is your liability coverage which relates to your auto insurance. It is the most the most important protection you can own to protect both your current and future lifestyles. Without this coverage and the proper amount, your financial future is at risk and very uncertain.

You have liability coverage for two reasons:

One is a moral and ethical obligation to restore someone you have harmed; and

The other is to protect your assets from someone suing you and taking them to pay for a loss for which you are responsible.

Without the proper coverage, everything you have and are saving for your future is at risk.

Let's say you or someone in your driving family get into an accident and injure or kill a surgeon.

How much do you think their spouse and children are going to need to make up for their income loss?

What about the loss of their lifetime capital potential?

They are going to hire a personal injury attorney and sue you for their loss and without protection, you may lose everything you have accumulated overnight.

A general belief is that having an auto policy and a homeowner's policy constitutes adequate property and liability coverage. When financial planning is done appropriately, we should be able to identify what policies are in place and the degree to which those policies provide adequate protection. In the event that shortcomings are identified, additional policies or policy endorsements can be implemented. A normal practice should be to pay particular attention to coverage options and policy limitations in order to tailor coverage for specific circumstances. Addressing your property and liability exposures, particularly with insurance, is a key part of the financial planning process which can help you avoid unnecessary losses. Insurance costs can be reduced through forgoing some insurance coverages or increasing deductibles; however, it may increase the need for a substantial emergency fund.

A loss exposure is the possibility that a loss could occur; however, the loss exposure addressed by property insurance is quite different from that addressed by liability insurance.

- A property loss exposure is the possibility that a person or organization will sustain a property loss resulting from the damaging, destruction, taking, or loss of use of property in which that person or organization has a financial interest.

- A liability loss exposure is the possibility of a claim alleging a person's or organization's legal responsibility for injury or damage suffered by another party.

There are two broad categories of property insurance: real property and personal property. Property insurance protects the property owners, not the property itself. In order for property insurance to perform properly, the owner must have an insurable interest in the property at the time the loss occurs. Additionally, the property owner could incur a financial injury due to loss of use of the property.

As an example, a driver may be forced to rent a car while his own car is being repaired due to an accident. Likewise, a family may incur expenses to live in a hotel while their house is being rebuilt, or a business may suffer a loss of income if the place of business has been damaged or destroyed. Property insurance is designed to cover losses that are a result of a covered peril.

Real property, is defined as land and anything that is growing on it, or affixed to it (i.e. buildings, fences, in-ground swimming pools, driveways, and retaining walls), and the bundle of rights that come with property ownership.

Personal property is defined to include anything that is subject to ownership other than real property. This includes such items as clothes, furniture, dishes, artwork, musical instruments, money, securities, airline tickets, office equipment, business inventory, vehicles, and boats. It also includes intangible property, such as copyrights and patents.

LIABILITY INSURANCE

The need for liability insurance arises out of the overly litigious nature of the U.S. legal environment. An individual can be sued for an amount that exceeds their life savings and potential future earnings for a momentary act of carelessness or negligence that creates injury or damage to another party. More of a concern is that the same individual can be sued by a claimant who alleges that the individual is responsible for the claimant's injury. Whether frivolous or not, the lawsuit itself can create hardship on the individual who has been sued. Fortunately, liability insurance is available both to cover defense costs and to pay damages awards for many types of claims.

Types of Liability Losses

Liability claims involve an alleged responsibility to pay damages. Damages can be categorized as compensatory damages or punitive damages:
- **compensatory damages** are designed to financially compensate or reimburse a claimant who has suffered a loss; and
- **punitive damages** are designed to punish a wrongdoer, or tortfeasor, whose outrageous conduct has caused another party to suffer a loss.

The primary design of liability insurance policies is to cover compensatory damages. Some policies exclude punitive damages, because the general thinking is that a wrongdoer is not really punished when the "punishment" is absorbed by their insurance.

The categories of liability losses that are typically covered by property and liability insurance are:
- bodily injury
- property damage
- personal injury
- contractual liability
- wrongful acts

Bodily injury occurs when a person suffers bodily harm, sickness, or disease. The injured party may incur such tangible losses as medical bills, lost income, or service procurement (i.e. cleaning the house or mowing the lawn). Bodily injury can also result in an award of damages for pain and suffering. In many cases, pain and suffering payments far exceed those paid for medical bills and lost income. Bodily injury can also result in claims by parties other than the person actively suffering the injury. For example, relatives can sue for wrongful death or loss of companionship.

Causing destruction or damage, even allegedly, to someone else's real or **personal property** can also result in a liability claim. The property damage can consist of actual damage to the property, but it can also arise because of lost income or extra expenses that result from the inability to use the property.

Personal injury (bodily injury) refers to a group of offenses that generally include libel, slander, invasion of privacy, and other offenses named in the policy, such as defamation or malicious prosecution.

Bases of Legal Liability

A liability claim occurs as the result of the alleged invasion of the legal rights of others. The invasion of such legal rights is a "legal wrong." The wrong can be criminal or civil. To be deemed a criminal wrong, the injury typically involves the public at large and is punishable by a governmental entity in the form of a fine and/or a jail term.

Torts and contracts are the basis of civil wrongs. Contracts can involve legal wrong when implied warranties are violated, bailee responsibilities are not fulfilled, or contractual obligations are breached. Torts are wrongs independent of contract (e.g. false imprisonment, assault, fraud, libel, slander, and negligence). Although governmental entities take action with respect to crime, civil injuries are remedied by court action instituted by the injured party in a civil action. The award of monetary damages is usually the remedy sought. The consequences of a crime are not usually insurable, but the liability for damages growing out of a civil wrong, are able to be insured.

Liability Insurance Umbrella

There are situations when an "umbrella" policy is not only necessary but also unforgiveable if you don't have one in place. You can purchase from your property and casualty agent when you purchase your auto and homeowners' coverage at a very low cost. Typically, when a person has considerable assets that they want to protect whose values are over-and-above the limits of their auto and homeowners' policies, they will implement umbrella coverage.

An example would be where one day your neighbor's child is playing with your kids in the pool and has a serious accident that requires extensive surgery and hospital stay. In the event that the parent is sued for damages caused by their child, the umbrella policy would protect their assets to the degree of the limits of the policy. Suppose your child is driving and runs a red light texting and runs into the surgeon we talked about earlier. Your chances of being sued are high and without an umbrella sufficient to cover the accident you will be responsible.

It is amazing how often we see people with significant assets in their Savings and Investment Tanks without an umbrella policy. The cost is very low for this coverage and when faced with legal action, the cost is next to nothing. You should not go another day without this protection.

WILLS & TRUSTS

Estate planning may be viewed as the conservation and distribution of a client's estate. However, a more accurate view is that estate planning is an integral part of financial planning, and the client's goal is to maximize their distributable wealth and transfer that wealth appropriately to their beneficiaries.

Three Primary Questions in Estate Planning
- Who should receive the client's property?
- How should beneficiaries receive the property?
- When should beneficiaries receive the property?

Once you have determined who should receive your property, you must then determine how your beneficiaries will receive the property. As an example property can be distributed outright to beneficiaries (in whole or in part) or the property can be left to beneficiaries in trust with various restrictions.

One example of a partial interest is a "life estate." The life estate gives the designated person the absolute right to possess, enjoy, and derive current income (e.g. rental income) from the property until the life estate ends.

You will generally need significant professional advice to answer the question of "how the estate should be transferred," but only you will be able to determine "when" your estate will be distributed.

A property can be owned entirely by one individual or interest can be shared jointly with multiple people. Joint ownership, may be in the form of Tenancy in Common, Joint Tenancy with Rights of Survivorship, or Tenancy by the Entirety. Property owned concurrently by two or more persons who may be (but are not necessarily) related is known as tenancy in common. Unless restricted by contract or agreement with the other co-owners, each tenant may dispose of his interest during his/her lifetime or at death. Joint tenancy with right of survivorship is similar to Tenancies In Common; however, the difference is that jointly-held property passes to the last surviving joint tenant, who, as sole surviving owner, has all rights in the property. A tenancy by The entirety is similar to a joint tenancy with right of survivorship although it is more restrictive because it is limited to property held jointly by a husband and wife. In practice, a tenancy by the entirety exists only during marriage and will be terminated upon divorce of the spouses.

Estate Planning Documents
- wills
- trusts
- durable powers of attorney
- advance medical directives

State intestacy provisions apply if an estate owner dies without having executed a valid will. In an intestacy situation, the state law is applied as a "substitute will" to establish the distribution of estate property to family members. The state legislature has really written the will for the decedent because he or she failed to draft one during life.

A properly drafted will can accomplish the following objectives:
- direct the disposition of the client's probate assets, (i.e. assets disposed through the probate process in the probate court in the county where the deceased person resided)
- nominate the personal representative of the testator (i.e. the executor/executrix) who will handle the administration of the client's estate
- determine the guardians of any minor children of the testator
- create testamentary trusts that will take effect at the testator's death to hold the property of the testator for the benefit of named beneficiaries
- name the trustee(s) of any trust(s) created under the will
- provide directions to the executor–executrix and/or trustees named in the will to define how these fiduciaries will manage assets contained in the estate or testamentary trust
- provide directions for payment of the estate's taxes and expenses
- establish the compensation of executors and/or trustees named in the will

A trust is a legal relationship in which one acts in a fiduciary capacity (position of trust) with respect to the property of another. The beneficial (or equitable interest) in the trust property is owned by the beneficiaries of the trust. The trustee has the duty to manage the trust property provided by the grantor for the benefit of the beneficiaries. A trust is often used to provide for beneficiaries when, for some reason, they are unable to administer the trust assets for themselves as in the case of a minor. The trust terms may be quite specific and restrictive and provide the trustee with very little discretion. For example, the terms may provide for specified distributions of income and/or principal to designated beneficiaries at various points in time.

A power of attorney is a written document that enables the client to designate an agent, known as the attorney-in-fact, to act on the client's behalf. The attorney-in-fact has the power to act on behalf of the client only with respect to powers specifically detailed in the document. A durable power of attorney remains valid and operative despite any subsequent incapacity of the client. A durable power of attorney takes effect immediately upon execution—though it may not be needed until much later, if ever. Some clients, however, are reluctant to grant another person wide powers to act when they themselves are still mentally and physically capable. Such clients might prefer a springing durable power of attorney lies dormant and ineffective until it is needed, typically upon the physical or mental incapacitation of the client. For example, a determination that the client has become incapacitated would trigger the springing power.

The advantages of a durable power of attorney include the following:
- An older client can execute a durable power of attorney and avoid the trouble and expense of having a guardian or a conservator appointed if the client loses legal capacity.
- The agent can be given the power to manage the client's assets should the client suffer a permanent or temporary loss of legal capacity. This is particularly important for owners of a closely held business.
- The durable power can replace or complement a revocable trust. The agent can manage a client's assets upon the client's legal disability and, if empowered, continue the client's dispositive scheme. For example, the agent could continue making annual gifts or charitable contributions after the client's legal incapacity but prior to the client's death.
- Most states allow a durable power of attorney for health care in which the agent can make medical care decisions on behalf of the client.

A durable power of attorney for health care (also known as an health care proxy) along with a living will are referred to as advance medical directives. By executing a durable power of attorney for health care clients are giving authority to some other person to carry out their health care instructions. A durable power of attorney for health care is a signed and witnessed legal document that names the person (attorney-in-fact) the client authorizes to make medical decisions about his care. The document then relieves family and friends of the responsibility for making decisions regarding life-prolonging actions.

A living will is another type of advance medical directive which describes the types of medical treatment a client wishes to receive or not receive. The living will communicates the client's medical wishes, should he/she become terminally ill and lie in a persistent vegetative state, unable to communicate. You should be aware that while a living will makes the client's medical wishes known, it does not guarantee those wishes will be followed. Someone still has to make medical decisions regarding whether or not to continue treatment. That person typically is the attorney-in-fact named in a durable power of attorney for health care to carry out the client's medical wishes as expressed in a living will. Together, these two types of advance medical directives are an important part of any estate or comprehensive financial plan.

Chapter 13:
Debt: What It Is and
What It Is Not

Y ou can't talk about money without talking about debt and the problems that come with it. Debt is a term that has different meanings in our world today and it is a term that is often misused.

Are you in debt if you have a loan? Many would say yes; you are in debt to the person or institution that loaned you money.

If you must make payments, are you in debt?

Are you in debt when you buy a house? Most would say that you are in debt to the lender for the amount of the loan until you have paid off the loan in full.

Are you in debt when you finance a car? Again, most people believe you are in debt until you have fully paid for the car.

What if what you believed to be true was not true? When would you want to know?

Let's begin with the question, "what creates debt?" The PEM may help you understand debt from a visual perspective. Let's talk about a major capital purchase first. A major capital purchase is any purchase that you can't afford to pay for in full with monthly cash flow. The key words are "in full." A major capital purchase requires more than the monthly income we have available to cover the expense and still pay our monthly bills. We run out of money before we run out of month. Of course, one option is to do without, cut back, but for many Americans that train has left the building long ago.

Some things just can't wait until we can save up the money. Your air conditioner goes out in July. You need a new set of tires on your car. A close relative passes away and you need to take off work without pay and purchase airfare for you and your family to attend. There are numerous things that qualify as a major capital purchase and a key thing to remember is they often come when least expected.

Assuming the expense is a necessity and your monthly cash flow is not enough for what you need, you have two options. One is to borrow money from yourself by draining from dollars you have put away earlier in your tanks to cover the expense. The other option is to borrow from a lender, like a bank or a credit card company and finance the cost over time with your current lifestyle cash flow.

If you borrow from yourself, using your own money, you will not have structured repayments but if you do not put the money back, you are robbing from your future because the money came from accounts you have previously set aside for that purpose. We will cover the concept of borrowing in chapter 14 called "Finance 101." Unfortunately, when we borrow from our future, sometimes our human nature can get the best of us and we don't get around to putting what we borrowed back which means we not only lost the money for our future but we also lost the interest that money would have earned.

For those who have nothing in their Savings and Investment Tanks, a major capital purchase poses an even bigger problem. With no access to capital, perhaps the only option available is to borrow using a credit card which does not require collateral, other than your job and the ability to pay. Notice that in both examples, each is borrowing and both borrowers have the same mindset to pay back the amount borrowed. Those that borrow from themselves have every intention to pay themselves back. Those that use a financial lender or credit card do not have a choice. With no access to capital, it is easier to slide even deeper into financial trouble having to pay exorbitant interest rates for a loan and still maintain ones current standard of living. It is interesting that when one expense comes, there are usually more to follow. The saying "when it rains it pours" makes a lot of sense. It is ironic that we borrow money to purchase something that supposedly would make our lifestyle better today but to pay for it, we must reduce our lifestyle in the future pay for it.

The use of credit cards is debt if you can't pay off the balance in full each month without being charged interest. If you pay the entire balance each month, it serves as a convenient method of carrying money and in today's world it is almost impossible to live without one. However, if everyone paid their balance off each month, the banks would not offer credit cards. If you don't pay it off in full each month, you are in debt because the amount you owe is not collateralized meaning you do not have the money to pay at the time of the transaction. There are very few things you can buy on a credit card that have the same economic value as they did when you paid for them. Most credit card purchases have little to no economic value once purchased. You can't give back your family vacation to Disney or your dinner at the Outback.

What makes using a credit card a problem is that without collateral, you are buying things with money you have yet to earn and with no guarantee you will have the ability to pay back what you have borrowed. You are spending some of your lifetime capital potential before you have the money in hand to pay for it. It would not be very efficient strategy to borrow money on a credit card and pay a higher interest rate to the bank than you are earning on your money. Again, people often find themselves in this position when they have no other access to capital.

Debt is an obligation on your future earnings. You lose the amount of money of the purchase and the interest that money could have earned had you saved it. You are a debtor to the creditor if you have no money in your tanks to pay what you owe. The loan does not make you a debtor, having no money in your tanks and depending on money you have yet to earn does. There can be no question that going into debt to pay for current lifestyle expenses is not a very efficient purchasing strategy.

The best way to pay for things if you are going to avoid going into debt is: pay cash. Many would say that the best way to pay for things if you don't like debt is to pay cash but there is a problem with paying cash. You are probably saying to yourself, "What in the world could be wrong with paying cash?"

To pay cash, one must first fill the tank, meaning they must be a saver, not spending every dollar they make which is a problem for many. Another problem is any interest earned on the money in your tank is taxable as gain which slows the growth of the account and finally, to pay cash you must drain the tank to make your purchase, thereby killing compound interest. So what could be better than paying cash?

So what if you could make your purchase without draining your tank?

What if you could make your purchase and your money could keep compounding interest uninterrupted? If you could do that, then where would you get the money to make your purchase?

To do that, you would collateralize a loan from a financial institution, securing the loan by pledging a portion of your account as collateral. A loan backed with collateral is not debt especially if your collateralized funds are larger than the amount borrowed and earning more interest than the interest charged on the loan. In the next chapter, we will discuss a very important economic principle which is you finance everything you buy.

Chapter 14:
Financing 101:
Pay Cash or Finance?

You may be thinking you don't need to read this chapter because you don't finance anything, you pay cash. If that is you, you especially of all people should not skip this chapter you probably should read this chapter twice. This chapter is crucial to everyone's financial success.

Here is a statement that may require you to think a little outside the box, a little uncommon wisdom. *You finance everything you buy.* When you read that statement, what was going through your mind? Perhaps you said to yourself, "that's not true. I pay cash for everything, I don't finance." Let me explain. You either pay interest or you give up the ability to earn interest. If you pay cash, you give up the opportunity those dollars in a tank could have earned. If you finance you pay interest but money in your tank continues to earn interest. One of the major reasons people pay cash is they do not want to pay interest because they see that as losing money. In reality you could be losing money if you pay cash because you must use dollars that could be in a tank you control that could be earning more interest than you would have to pay if you financed.

This is a concept you are going to have to think your way through but follow closely. You lost the interest you would have earned had you left the money in the tank. In other words, you personally financed the purchase using your own money. Now you have to earn more income, those dollars must flow through the Tax Filter and then be pumped back into the account from which you took the money to get back to the place you were in before your cash purchase. You self-financed the purchase.

When people tell me the reason they pay cash is that they don't like paying interest. I respond by saying, "you must like losing interest." Of course, they are puzzled by that statement but you should understand what I am saying. If you pay cash, you gave up the opportunity to earn interest on those dollars which means you lost interest.

The money you pumped into your Savings and Investment Tanks are dollars being set aside for your future lifestyle requirements, not to spend on your current lifestyle desires. Even if you are putting away enough to secure your financial future, draining a tank for a current lifestyle expense means you must give up control of those dollars. Control of your money may be even more valuable than the return on your money. When you take money from your accounts without paying them back at interest, you are effectively robbing from your future for something you need or want today. It is your money but you should understand that it comes at a cost, loss of interest you could earn and control.

Since you do not have structured payments when you borrow from yourself, you may not feel the pressure to repay the amount you borrowed, but you should. Remember if you do not put the money back, you will have lost not only the dollars borrowed but the interest you would have earned had you left the money in your account. If you borrow money from yourself, you should put back not only the money taken but the interest you lost while the money was out. How often have you done that? Before you finance a current lifestyle expense by draining your tank, it would be wise to see if there is another opportunity to finance your purchase using OPM (other people's money). It may not always be possible but preferably you would want to borrow at a lower rate than you are earning on your money.

The interest rate is not the only factor to consider. Even if the rate to borrow is the same or higher than you are earning, you need to determine if access to the money is worth the added interest expense. Once you have spent the money it may take considerable time to get back to where you were.

When you come to the realization that every dollar spent on current lifestyle has an economic impact on your future, it should change how you look at everything you buy. Money spent on your current lifestyle is enjoyed and gone forever, never to return and those dollars spent also have a cost greater than themselves. You must calculate the time value of that dollar or the opportunity cost to fully understand the dollar's true value.

Let me prove this concept to you visually with the PEM. When you borrow from yourself you have to drain the tank. To get back to where you were, you will have to earn additional income. That money must flow through the Tax Filter and the after tax dollars can then be pumped up the Future Savings Tube back into the tank you took the money from to get you back to where you were before you borrowed the money. It is financing, it is called self-financing. You finance everything you buy.

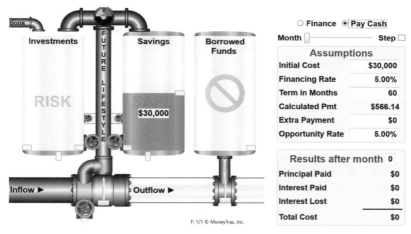

To make the purchase you must drain the tank. In this example you had $30,000 in your tank and you drained the tank and spent the money.

Now you must put the money back plus the interest you lost while the money was out of your account to get back to the same financial position.

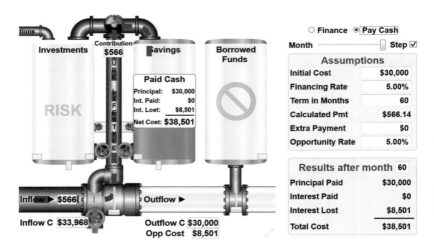

Another critical thing to remember is that every dollar not saved is gone forever, never to return.

So before you make any major capital purchase, you need to consider the cost and not just the sticker price, but the opportunity cost as well. The real issue is not what you buy, but how to pay for it. The PEM will help you determine if you can or should make the purchase. Just because you can does not necessarily mean you should.

In determining "what" you can afford to buy, one of your first considerations should be do you have the monthly cash flow to cover the monthly payments from your current lifestyle cash flow without draining money from a tank to pay for it. Secondly, you should ask yourself if the purchase will require you to reduce the money you are putting into your Future Lifestyle Tanks to get it.

This is not to say you should not buy the things you want or those things that bring joy and happiness to your life. If you are putting away enough money in the tanks for you to live like you desire in the future and you don't have to drain a tank or reduce your contributions into the tanks, you should feel the freedom to enjoy the resources you have earned. You have a balanced economic model. A wonderful thing about having a balanced Personal Economic Model is that it allows you to enjoy your current lifestyle purchases knowing that the purchase is not keeping you from being able to put away the money you will need to live just as you live today in the future adjusted for inflation. Knowing that you are well balanced financially for tomorrow can make the life you live today even more pleasant and meaningful.

Now that you understand paying cash is financing and that you finance everything you buy, you have two choices when you wish to make a major capital purchase. You can drain a tank and self-finance or finance using OPM or other people's money and maintain liquidity use and control of your money.

The Private Reserve Strategy in Chapter 20 will provide insight into how you can find the most efficient way to finance your current lifestyle desires allowing your money to compound interest uninterrupted and to remain in control of your money.

Let's do some math to help you see what I am talking about. Suppose you had $30,000 in your tank earning 5 %. At the end of a five year period, you would have earned $8,501 in interest. No big surprise here. Now suppose that you drained the tank to pay cash for a car. How much did the car cost you? If you said $30,000, you are not correct because you forgot to include the time value of money or the opportunity cost on the purchase. The car costs $38,501 over five years. The cost of the car is not just the sales price of the car, but you must also calculate the value of the money spent or what it would have been worth had you kept it in the tank earning 5% interest, in this example.

If you do not apply opportunity cost, paying cash will always seem like to best way to go. At first glance, it looks like you will lose $8,501 in interest if you finance and that sounds unacceptable. However, since you took $30,000 out of your tank that was earning you 5% you could have left it in the tank and earned $8,501. This is why we said that if you don't like paying interest, you must like losing interest.

How would you like to pay for it?

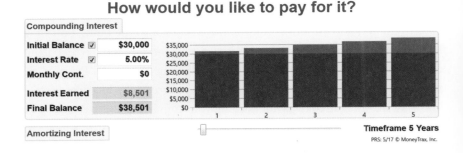

If buying a car, or any purchase, costs the same if you pay cash or if you finance it over time, which option would you choose? Let's continue talking about buying a car.

The first question you should ask yourself is: can I buy the car? Do you have the money in a tank to pay for it in full? If you don't have enough then you can't self-finance, you only have one option which is to finance with OPM. Let's assume you have enough in your tanks to drain it by the amount of the purchase. Great, then the next thing you should be asking yourself is, are there opportunities for me to get the car using OPM at a lower rate than I am earning on my money allowing me to maintain control of my capital? If you are earning more interest than you would have to pay to use OPM, why would you choose to lose interest and give up control of your money? If the money in your tank is not earning enough for you to use OPM, perhaps you need to think about having your money in another tank.

Let's put some numbers to that discussion. One option would be to pay cash for a $30,000 car and "self-finance" putting back the money over time.

You have a $30,000 car in the driveway but your tank is down $30,000 and you have lost access and control of that amount of money until you put it back. It is interesting that we would never think to miss a car payment to the bank but we do not feel the same when we borrow our own money.

Another option is for you to maintain control of your $30,000 and borrow from a financial institution using their money. You finance the car and with a loan to the lender with monthly payments. Would you consider this person in debt? It is not but it would be debt if they had nothing in their tanks. In this option, you would have a $30,000 car sitting in your garage with monthly payments and $30,000 still sitting in your tank earning interest to which you have access and control. Either way, you have payments. In option one, you have payments to your future; with option two, you have payments to a lender paid from your current lifestyle cash flow and your future is still as solid as it was before the purchase.

In option one if you self-finance you gave away $30,000 of your collateral and bought a car which you could have purchased with your signature using the car as collateral rather than your money. If the interest rate you are earning is the same as the interest rate to finance, the car will cost you the same either way. In chapter 20, we will discuss in detail the importance of maintaining your collateral capacity through a strategy called the private reserve.

How would you like to pay for it?

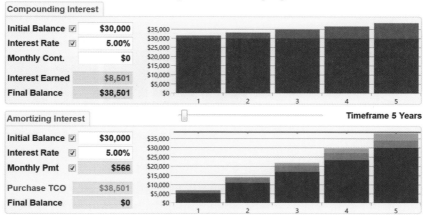

PRS: 5/17 © MoneyTrax, Inc.

This calculation illustrates the fact that if you financed the car in this example over five years, your monthly payments would be $566. $566 a month compounded at 5% over five years would be $38,501. I realize this is a head scratcher but you must understand this concept. If you pay cash, you had to remove the money from your tank that was earning 5%. The interest you lost to use your money and self-finance must be added to the cost of the purchase. In addition to paying cash you also lost control of $30,000 until you get around to putting it back. Now you must earn more money, it must flow through the Tax Filter and then you must pump it back into your account earning 5% to get back to where you were before you made your purchase. How many times do you want your money flowing through the Tax Filter?

There is one more thing to add to this discussion. Many are under the misconception that if they pay extra on a loan, it will reduce the cost of the loan. Let's assume that you decided to pay an extra $200 a month on the car loan beginning the very first payment.

How would you like to pay for it?

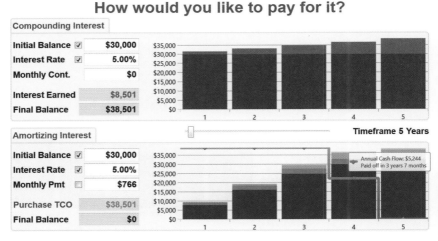

Your required payment is only $566 a month but you decided to pay $766 a month to pay the loan off faster. You will notice that the car loan would be paid off in 3 years and 7 months, 29 months early. It is a wonderful feeling to have no more payments but notice that the cost of the loan is still $38,501.

To pay off the loan early, you must give the lender *extra* money that you could have just as easily put into your tank that was earning 5% for you. Extra money is dollars over and above what you need to cover your normal current lifestyle expenses. The amount you saved by paying the loan off quicker is exactly the same amount you would have had if you had taken those same dollars and put them in your tank. You gave away extra cash flow today to free up extra cash flow later.

The car costs the same if you pay cash or if you finance, assuming the interest rate you can earn on your money is the same as the interest rate you must pay to finance the purchase, even if you pay extra. What changed was your cash flow. Obviously, if you can earn 5% on your money and pay less interest by using other people's money, you would never drain the tank and lose interest and in addition give up control of your money. If the interest rate on the loan is greater than the interest you are earning you would need to consider if the value of the interest difference is greater than the value of maintaining control and access to your money.

Worksheet Viewer

Print | Export | Zoom 100 % ⌄

Amortization and Compounding Schedule

Year	Annual Interest Paid	Cumulative Interest Paid	Annual Interest Earned	Cumulative Interest Earned	Cumulative Interest Differential	EOY Loan Balance	EOY Capital Balance	Cumulative Principal Payments	Amortization Principal at Interest	Amortization Interest at Interest	Amortization Total Cost of Ownership
1	$1,376.99	$1,376.99	$1,534.86	$1,534.86	$157.87	$24,583.34	$31,534.86	$5,416.66	$5,541.39	$1,410.13	$6,951.51
2	$1,099.86	$2,476.85	$1,613.38	$3,148.24	$671.39	$18,889.56	$33,148.24	$11,110.44	$11,649.79	$2,608.89	$14,258.68
3	$808.56	$3,285.40	$1,695.93	$4,844.17	$1,558.77	$12,904.47	$34,844.17	$17,095.53	$18,368.73	$3,570.97	$21,939.70
4	$502.35	$3,787.75	$1,782.69	$6,626.86	$2,839.11	$6,613.17	$36,626.86	$23,386.83	$25,744.67	$4,269.02	$30,013.69
5	$180.47	$3,968.22	$1,873.90	$8,500.76	$4,532.54	$0.00	$38,500.76	$30,000.00	$33,827.27	$4,673.49	$38,500.76

When you look at the value of your money including the opportunity cost, it should bring a new perspective to the things you buy with your hard earned cash. This is not to say that you should not enjoy your purchases but it should give you pause to think about what it really costs to have them. Don't forget the lifetime capital potential discussion. Every dollar you earn has the potential to be more than the dollar itself. When you spend the dollar on your current lifestyle, you lose the dollar plus what it could have earned had you saved it.

Let's look at this information from a different angle. Say that you are out looking at cars. You "want" a car that costs $50,000 and when you consider the cost from your present age 40 to your age 65, it will cost you almost $215,000 assuming a 6% return (6% is your opportunity cost rate since you have money in your Investment Tank earning that amount). Now you understand that is a lot of money but you "need" a new car, so you look at a $30,000 car which will cost you $129,000 over the same time period. You have the cash flow to buy the $50,000 car, but if you get that car, you will not be able to fully fund your Savings and Investment accounts. You can now make a more informed financial decision based on your understanding of the true cost. If you purchase the $30,000 car, it will allow you to continue putting away what you need for retirement, giving you $85,000 more at your retirement age than you will have if you make the $50,000 car purchase. If you can continue doing what you need to do for your future without having to drain a tank or reduce your contributions into the tanks, then you can make the purchase with the peace of mind knowing that your decision today is not putting you in an undesirable financial position for your future. Your Personal Economic Model is getting closer to being in balance.

Living with *your* Personal Economic Model in balance is a desirable financial position because it relieves the financial pressure life today can bring, as well as providing the security that you will be able to handle the financial pressures of tomorrow giving you unrestricted control of your money.

You are going to need to buy things as long as you live; so let's look at three different ways that people buy, borrow, and pay for major capital purchases searching for the most efficient way to do each.

The Debtor works to spend. They have no savings; they do not earn interest, they pay interest. Since they have no money in their tanks, they find themselves living from pay check to pay check, month to month, paying others interest to fund their current lifestyle. These folks live with the fear that something could come along where they would not be able to pay their bills because their only source of capital is the money they have yet to earn. They have the potential to pay if they don't lose their job, their car doesn't break down, if they don't get sick, or don't become disabled. Unfortunately many people in America live under this kind of stress every day.

The Saver saves to avoid paying interest. These folks do not like paying interest on any purchase. They save, they earn interest, and they pay cash for their purchases. Some savers are more interested in not paying interest than earning interest. When they need something, they drain the tank and pay cash and begin working to fill the tank again. They feel secure when they have money in their tank but when they have to drain the tank to make their purchases it can create a great deal of financial stress, especially if the purchase leaves their tank balance near zero. Unfortunately, from time to time, they are forced to repeat the process of saving for later and having to drain the tank for current lifestyle expenses. This strategy is certainly better than the debtor but leaves the saver frustrated often feeling they can never get ahead.

The Wealth Creator saves—they earn a reasonable rate of return on their money, and they collateralize lifestyle purchases using other people's money utilizing the money in their tanks to secure a loan. The wealth creator has a good handle on the four financial questions answered with the Lifestyle Regulator and is focused on maintaining a balanced financial model. They are pumping enough up the Future Lifestyle Tube to be able to live at retirement like they live today adjusted for inflation. They also must make major capital purchases like the debtor and saver but they use their collateral and borrow against their money, rather than from it continuing to earn compound interest uninterrupted and remain in control. Since they have money (collateral), they can afford to shop for the most favorable interest rate available to finance their purchase. Their desire is to borrow money at a lower interest rate than their money is earning and because they can use their money as collateral, they qualify for the best rates. They also have excellent credit which can provide opportunities to borrow using a signature loan without giving up their collateral on many purchases.

When the Debtor borrows, they borrow from a lender, usually at the highest market rates because they have poor credit or no collateral other than their future earning potential.

When the Saver borrows, they borrow from their own account and pay cash. They self-finance. Remember paying cash is financing, it is self-financing. Each time they take money from their account that is earning interest, they reset compounding on the amount of money taken. They have every intention to put back the money they borrowed against their future but often human nature gets the best of them. Unfortunately, other things pop up that need their financial attention and they never get around to putting the money back. If they do put the money back, they rarely put back the interest they lost while the money was out of their account, reducing the amount of money they will have available in the future.

The Wealth Creator borrows from a lender at negotiated rates using their money as collateral to continue earning compound interest on their future life-style savings and investment dollars. They finance current lifestyle purchases and fund their future lifestyle accounts. If they can finance without giving up collateral, that is preferable when possible. They also determine the real cost of every major capital purchase and the opportunity cost before they buy. They understand that what they do today will make or break their tomorrows.

When it comes time to pay for major capital purchases, the Debtor has few options and is often stuck paying the lender at the highest market rates. Unfortunately, this is a dangerous position because with insufficient cash flow and no reserves the interest rates charged can drive the debtor even deeper into debt and closer to bankruptcy.

The Saver pays cash but has payments as well which often go unnoticed. They have payments to the account from which they took the money in order for them to get back to the same position they were in before they made the purchase. An even bigger issue is that even if they put the money back, few put back the interest they would have earned while they had their money out of the tank, thus putting more pressure on their future.

You might say to yourself if my money is earning a lower interest rate than I will have to pay to finance with a lender, it makes sense to drain the tank and self-finance. The question you should be asking is why do you have money in that tank? Perhaps you need to look at better return opportunities that are available that still offer liquidity use and control of your money. If your money is in the safe tank you should look for safe account alternatives that can provide more return still with no risk of loss as well as more bene-fits. Obviously risk is an issue so you would want to have your money in a position that provides the interest potential you desire at the risk level you are willing to take that can also provide additional benefits besides just return.

The Wealth Creator makes payments to a chosen lender, allowing their money to earn uninterrupted compound interest and maximizing benefits. We will discuss in detail how to do this in chapter 20 with the discussion of the private reserve.

I would like to tell you a story called The Zero Line that may help bring into focus what we just discussed and how important it is to maximize efficiencies in how we handle our money.

The Zero Line represents a financial position where you have nothing and you owe nothing. Financially speaking you are at Zero. I remember the day I graduated from college. I had everything I owned, which was not much, in the trunk of my car. I had no money; I had nothing other than my lifetime capital potential. You could say I was at the Zero Line. Fortunately, I did not have a student loan which would have placed me well below the Zero Line on graduation day. Many of our students today are saddled with a tremendous amount in student loans. Our children are owned by the federal government and financial institutions that loaned them money to pay for their education.

The lenders loaned the money to those who would be able to get a job, pay taxes, and earn an income so they could pay back the principal and interest on their loans. It seems like a good plan to loan money to educated individuals who most likely will want to work and will make enough money to be able to pay back what they borrow. This is a huge problem for our children and one too complicated to cover everything you need to know in this book. Suffice it to say, many of our children who graduate from college with student loans are beginning their life well below The Zero Line. The cost of education is one of the top five major wealth transfers and we will give you some thoughts on how to minimize this expense in chapter 18.

So you graduate from college or go straight to work out of high school. You find employment and you have a steady income for the first time in your life. Your first major capital purchase is…a car. You have no money in your tanks, so you finance a car with an institution that will take a risk on you using your job and the car as collateral. Remember that all loans require collateral. The collateral for your student loan was that big tank called your Lifetime Capital Potential. You are driving to work now in a new car and making principal and interest payments each month, working your way back to… zero.

Okay, so you have the car. You are making your payments on time and life is good. It is about to get even better; you have found someone to journey with through life together. Now you have two incomes, but two car payments and maybe even two student loans. You now find yourself even further behind struggling even harder to get to Zero. Then kids come along, requiring a larger house, bigger cars that require $500 car seats for each of your three kids and it is easy to see why you haven't taken a vacation in ten years and your brain is so fried that you believe that taking the kids to Disney World and maxing out your credit card actually makes sense. They did not put all that in the brochure.

This picture looks like too many in America but there is only one way to get on the other side of Zero and that is to save; to fill those two tanks. It makes sense and sounds impossible but it isn't. Knowing what it takes is the first step in making it happen. Most want to do something about it but the only option they know is to give up something or do without and that does not seem possible. It is so easy to get caught up in what it costs to live today that you forget or ignore the fact that you are also responsible for what it is going to cost you to live tomorrow.

The Savers have learned to balance their current lifestyle desires with their current cash flow and put money away for the unexpected in perhaps what many would call an emergency fund. Isn't it interesting how many emergencies and things you just can't live without pop up when you have money in your emergency fund? The Saver definitely has less financial stress than the Debtor but is still stressed knowing they are not doing enough to secure their future. They must drain a tank to cover the unexpected events that life brings our way which resets compounding each time they use their money. They are doing something but deep down, they know it is not working and not going to be enough.

The Wealth Creators have learned to balance their current lifestyle desires with their future lifestyle requirements. They do not spend everything they make. They are also savers and investors. They begin their financial journey with the end in mind understanding that they alone are responsible for the life they will live during their later years as well as today. They are steadfast in their efforts to fill the tanks. They pay themselves first. They understand the importance of having access to capital and know the value of uninterrupted compound interest. They use OPM to pay for their current lifestyle and collateralizing their loans if necessary against their savings and investment dollars while continuing to earn interest to advance their future. They understand that interest rates will vary over time and rates of return come and go but control of their money is most important. They take advantage of opportunities for increased returns cautiously while protecting their underlying assets. They understand the fact that you finance everything you buy and that although they could easily pay cash, those dollars have an opportunity cost as well. They look for opportunities to be more efficient with their dollars by first avoiding unnecessary losses before considering those that potentially promise higher returns.

The Wealth Creators build for the future and when their current lifestyle cash flow is not enough to cover a major capital expense, they borrow against their money and finance the purchase paying for it over time with monthly cash flow or they hold off on the purchase.

Again let me remind you that the focus of this book is to help you be more efficient by avoiding unnecessary losses. How you pay for things can have a huge impact on your cash flow and how much you will have in the future. Before looking for investments that promise higher returns we believe the best use of your time is to avoid potential losses. In the next few chapters, we will look at the top five areas where you may experience financial loss and we will give you strategies to help you avoid, minimize, or eliminate those losses where possible.

Chapter 15: Mortgages: Making the Right Choice

While there are many areas where potential unnecessary losses can occur, we will focus on the top five areas where the largest losses occur with the first being Mortgages.

How you pay for your house can have a big impact on your financial future. There is a great deal more to buying a house than picking out where you want to live and how much of a monthly payment you can afford. There are numerous mortgage options offered by the lending institutions and that fact means they make more on some loans than they do on others. If they made the same amount on every mortgage loan they would only have one.

Before we get into this conversation, it would be wise to remember what we have learned from earlier lessons in the PEM about money:

1: You finance everything you buy.

2: Paying cash is financing, it is self-financing.

3: The cost does not go down when you pay extra on a loan.

4: You must calculate the time value of money or opportunity cost on every dollar.

Your house is a major capital purchase and we are of the opinion that everyone should have their home paid off and paid off as fast as possible—but choosing the right loan and the most efficient way to accomplish that can be confusing, as there is more than one way to pay off your house. We encourage you to make decisions based on what is true, not necessarily what you believe to be true.

Disclaimer: We don't recommend that anyone take equity from their house to purchase any savings or investment product. It is our opinion that if you are advised to cash out home equity to buy a financial product, you are not getting good advice.

This discussion will help you separate fact from fiction, so that you can learn how to pay off your house in the fastest and safest manner allowing you to be in control of the entire process. By the end of this discussion, you may learn a few things about Mortgages that could change how you look at your money for the rest of your life. I promise this information will be uncommon.

Before we get too far, let's take a little True or False quiz about mortgages.

A large down payment will save you more money on your mortgage over time than a small down payment.

A 15-year mortgage will save more money over time than a 30-year mortgage.

Making extra principal payments saves you money.

The interest rate is the main factor in determining the cost of a mortgage.

You are more secure having your home paid off than financed one hundred percent.

If you answered "True" to any of these questions, you will want to turn the TV off and start paying closer attention to what you are about to read.

Here are a few more questions that might help you look at how you pay for your house in a different way.

If you pay extra on your mortgage loan, does the value of your house go up? No

If you pay extra, do your payments go down? No

If you need the extra money back, can you get to it easily? No and not without cost.

What will your kids do with your house when you are gone? They will sell the house.

As we work our way through this chapter we will introduce you to three couples, all with the same goal of having a house that is paid for, and all believing that the way they are going about doing it is the best way. We will look at each couple and how their mortgage decisions impact many different areas of their financial life.

Mortgage lenders commonly spend their time focusing only on the payment amount and interest rate. While these factors are important, there are several other factors that should also be considered. To help you understand how these factors might ultimately impact you, let's look in on our three fictitious couples.

The first couple is the Free-n-Clears. They purchased their house with cash. They own their house free and clear. For many this is the American dream, position A, no mortgage and no monthly payments.

The second couple is the Owe-it-Alls. They have enough money to pay cash for their house, like the Free-n-Clears, but decided to keep their money in a safe account (green tank), taking no risk with this money. They chose not to self-finance but rather, finance with a mortgage lender and secured a mortgage loan. They like the fact that they have complete access to their money in case they ever needed it and because they can pay off their loan any day they wish they believe their house is paid off as well. They believe that having a mortgage loan is a great thing because it allows them to be in control of their money. They can easily pay their monthly mortgage payment from their current lifestyle. They also feel that they can earn at least the same or greater interest than the interest they are paying for their mortgage loan especially with the tax deduction they receive on the interest portion of the loan. They understand that the house will increase in value over time with or without a mortgage loan on the property. They were able to secure a loan for 100% of the value of the house at the time of purchase. (These loans are not available currently).

The third couple is the Pay-Extras. They chose a 15 year loan that allows them to make larger principal payments every month than a 30 year loan with the goal of paying their loan off as soon as they can so they too can be Free-N-Clear. They even make extra payments on their 15 year loan. They would have liked to have paid cash but did not have enough money to do that when they bought the house.

The Free-n-Clears and the Owe-it-Alls are at either end of the spectrum and the Pay-Extras are right in the middle. Looking at this topic from both extremes will give you clarity in determining where you are in this conversation and which way you are going. We think you will learn a great deal from these three couples and develop your own opinion as we answer the questions mentioned earlier and many more as you work your way through this chapter in determining the most efficient way to pay for your house.

For our discussion, we will assume The Free-n-Clears, the Pay-Extras and the Owe-it-Alls live next door to one another in identical homes with identical values. So which of these couples do you think is in the best financial position today and for their future? Which couple is most like you?

We will explore the many issues, one by one that impact mortgage decisions to find out which couple you think is on the right track.

Inflation

One area people often forget to consider when financing is inflation. Inflation tells us that the dollars you have today will be less valuable in the future. Suppose you have a fixed payment today of $2,000 a month, what will that same $2,000 buy in 10, 20, or 30 years?

Let's assume you currently have a 30-year fixed loan with a payment of $2,000 a month and an inflation rate of 3%. In 30 years, $2,000 will only buy $823.97 of goods. The check you write today for $2,000 is worth $2,000. The $2,000 check you write in year 30 will only be worth $823.97. The mortgage payments you make in the early years of your mortgage are the most valuable dollars you will ever earn.

Would it be better to give the bank your most valuable dollars or your least? Wouldn't it be great if you could sign 360 checks at the closing and the bank not cash them until the final day of your 30-year loan? You can't but you get the picture.

So let's check-in on the couples and see how inflation is impacting them.

The Free-n-Clears gave control of their most valuable dollars to the seller up front and now will have to qualify to access any of the dollars they used to purchase the house and pay to get them. Interest rates in the future may be greater than current rates are today if and when they need to access their equity. They are not paying interest but the money in their house is not earning interest either. The house will appreciate the same if they have it paid off or financed 100%. They look at a mortgage loan as debt and they are glad they have this debt out of the way.

The Pay-Extras voluntarily give the bank their most valuable extra dollars on top of their required mortgage payment every chance they get, giving up control of those dollars and losing the interest they could have earned had they put the extra money in their tanks in an account they own and control. They see their loan as debt and want to get out of debt as soon as possible.

The Owe-it-Alls have a fixed payment 30-year loan that allows them to give the bank payments that are worth less and less each month—while keeping their money in their tanks earning interest offsetting the impact of inflation. They believe that over time, they can earn a higher interest rate on their money than their mortgage loan rate while maintaining access to 100% of their capital. They do not believe their mortgage loan is debt because they have the money to pay off their loan any day they wish. Besides, the house is worth the same amount of their loan and the house will appreciate over time allowing them to sell the house and never be in debt. You can't be in debt if your house is worth more than you owe.

Key Concept: Your home actually costs you more the faster you pay it off because you are using your most valuable dollars

Down Payments

One of the main reasons many people like to make large down payments on their house purchase is to lower their payments to save interest. Does your down payment earn any interest? No. Any access to equity would need to be above the amount of down payment required. Remember the term "opportunity cost." You only have two options when financing. One is to self-finance by paying cash, giving up the interest you were earning or could have earned and giving up the control of your money as well. Option two is to keep your money earning interest and finance the purchase using other people's money, preferably at a lower rate than you are earning on the money in your account putting you in control.

The largest down payment you can make is to pay cash, which is what the Free-n-Clears did. They have no payments and no access to their money. To gain access to their money, they will have to go through the mortgage loan process to get to it. They will have to qualify to get to their own money.

Key Concept: opportunity cost — if you lose a dollar that you did not have to lose, you not only lose that dollar but you also lose what that dollar could have earned for you had you been able to keep it. If you pay off your loan, you are saving interest but you are losing interest as well because you could have put those same dollars in your tank.

What would the Free-n-Clears down payment be worth, had they been able to keep it and invest it compared to what will their house be worth over the same period? Let's put some math behind this concept and take a deeper look.

Assume each of the couples houses are worth $300,000.

The Free-n-Clears made the biggest down payment possible—which was the entire $300,000.

The Pay-Extras did not have enough to pay cash although they wanted to, so they pay extra by choosing a 15-year loan. They chose the 15 year loan over the 30 year loan to pay their house off quicker. In effect, they are accelerating the principal payments required by choosing the shorter mortgage loan option.

The Owe-it-Alls put down the least amount, zero down—and financed as long as possible with a 30-year mortgage and have $300,000 in a tank they control and live in a house that is worth $300,000, never wishing to pay extra principal payments on their mortgage loan. When they have extra money to put away they put it in a tank that they own and control, not their house. They understand that the house will not go up in value if they pay more on their loan.

Assuming an investment rate of 8%, (for illustrative purpose only) the $300,000 that the Owe-it-Alls invested would grow to be worth $3,280,719 in 30 years. If they could borrow the $300,000 at a lower rate, they would keep the difference.

The $300,000 in the Free-n-Clears house earned no interest. So, if the Free-n-Clears can't sell their house in 30 years for $3,280,719—they made a minor financial error. Money in your house does not compound interest; it appreciates or depreciates. The value of their house will be the same if they have their house paid in full or financed 100%. The Free-n-Clears are happy that their other investment dollars are earning 8% but the money in their house is earning zero. It would be hard to call anything with zero return a great investment. They never think about the fact that they could have financed their house at 3.5% and qualified for interest deductions making their cost to borrow even less. They also never think about the fact that if they could earn the same amount of interest or more than the cost of the loan after tax, they could control the money.

The Pay-Extras did not have enough to pay their house off at the closing or they would have done so. The fact that they are paying extra means they are moving in the direction of the Free-n-Clears as fast as they can. It would not make much sense to put extra money on their mortgage loan at 3.5% if they could put those same dollars in an account that could potentially earn them 8% but they are doing it anyway. They give up extra cash flow today to have extra cash flow later. Unfortunately they are giving up control to do it. They want to get out of debt as fast as they can. When they purchased the house they put 20% down and they have been making payments. They gave the bank $60,000 at the closing and their house is worth $300,000. They can't be in debt because their house is worth more than they owe.

Investment Opportunities

Rather than paying cash for their house, the Owe-it-Alls have $300,000 invested in an account they own and control earning more interest than their monthly mortgage payment. They understand that mortgage interest rates rise and fall over time and if rates drop lower than their current loan rate, they will refinance. They like having a monthly mortgage payment because it allows them to control their money and they can easily cover the monthly mortgage payment with their current lifestyle cash flow. If they should ever have a bad cash flow month, they can access the money in their account to help with unexpected expenses. They also qualify for a deduction on the interest portion of their payment which the Free-n-Clears do not get and the Pay-Extras are reducing with each extra payment. The tax advantage of the interest deduction reduces the total cost to borrow which is a bonus which the Free-n-clears and the Pay-Extra's are missing out on. If the government were to take the interest deduction away, the Owe-it-Alls would still want a mortgage loan in order to maintain control of their money.

The Free-n-Clears, put $300,000 down—giving away the control of the money to the seller of their house but in their mind, they are able to invest the cash flow they now have available since they have no mortgage payments. If you already have your house paid off, this is a good strategy. We would never encourage anyone to cash out and invest their equity in anything. However, if you are looking at which way to go before you buy, you may want to think about it a little more before you close. The money currently in the house earns zero; so before you pay cash, consider the opportunity cost of having those dollars sit idle until you sell. The house is going to appreciate the same, no matter how much money they have in it. However, since they do not receive mortgage interest deductions, our couple will have to assume a higher investment risk than the Owe-it-Alls on their investment dollars. It is interesting that once the house is paid off, people want to then look for places to invest that offer deductions. They are doing one thing that is killing tax deductions and once their mortgage loan is paid off, they want to look for an investment account that will provide tax deductions. Strange but true.

So with the understanding that money used for down payments earns no interest, is subject to the ups and downs of the mortgage market, and reduces tax deductions, what is the ideal amount to put down when purchasing a home? Nothing! That's right. Zero! Zilch! Nada! Unfortunately, that is no longer possible today but you should understand that the least amount down is as close as you can get in today's economy.

Key Concept: If you finance with a lending institution, you transfer interest for the privilege of using their money. If you pay cash, or self-finance, you save interest, but you lose interest as well, because that money is not earning anything for you.

Your Home as an Investment

Many people today consider their home one of their largest investments. Let's see if it is a good place to put your money.

Assume that the homes of all three of our couples have appreciated over the 10 years since their purchase and they are all worth $390,000 today. When they moved in their houses they were worth $300,000. Each has also put an additional $25,000 into improving their properties making their rate of return in the neighborhood of 2.64%. Would you consider this a good investment return? When you add in property taxes, the cost of homeowners insurance, and maintenance, the rate of return is much less and possibly negative.

The Free-n-Clears feel they are doing pretty well but have never calculated the internal rate of return. They like having no mortgage payments and they feel pretty good because their house is appreciating. They have other dollars invested that are doing quite well.

The Pay-Extras feel the same way but both are shocked to learn their internal rate of return is around 2.64%. They said they were earning around 8% in their other investments but 2.64% does not sound very good.

The Owe-it-Alls have been able to earn their investment return on their $300,000 lump sum which is more interest than their monthly mortgage payment and their house is appreciating just like the other couples across the street. If their $300,000 earned 4% their account value would have grown to $444,073.29 and their house is now worth $390,000. They are very pleased also.

You will notice that your house is not in the investment or savings tank in the PEM. It is a current lifestyle expense. While it is the only lifestyle expense that can potentially return money to the model, the money in your house does not earn interest and it certainly does not compound interest uninterrupted. Another reason it is not in the Savings or Investment Tanks is to get the money to invest in another opportunity you must sell the house. Once sold, you can put the money in either tank you choose but you will then need to find a new place to sleep. Sleeping inside costs you money, no matter how you pay for it.

Appreciation

You may be thinking we forgot that your house could be appreciating. It does not earn interest but it does appreciate or depreciate. While history would say that your house would normally appreciate, it is too early to forget about 2006-2008 when property values plummeted across the nation.

Remember the Free-n-Clears, the Pay-Extras and the Owe-it-Alls live next door to one another in identical homes with identical values. Whose house will appreciate the fastest?

The fact is they will all appreciate exactly the same. Paying cash, making larger down payments or extra monthly payments, or a house with a mortgage of 100% of the house value, does not make one house worth more than the other. Since that is true, then which option puts you in the safest position? Which option offers you the most control of your money?

Key Concept: Your home appreciates the same whether you have it paid off or financed 100%.

Depreciation:

If the value of the house goes down how do our couples fair?

The Free-n Clears are probably not even concerned although it may take some time for the mortgage market to bounce back. Should they need access to their equity the amount of dollars available would be less and mortgage interest rates could be more. If they had to sell they would lose money.

The Pay-Extras might be troubled to keep putting extra money on a house that is worth less now than they originally paid for it. This was a big problem in 2007 and 2008 which had many people walking away from their loans leaving the bank to take the loss. If they are forced to sell they could potentially lose all the extra money they put in the house.

The Owe-it-Alls are in the same boat but remember they still have their money and access to it. Access to capital is not a problem and with mortgage interest rate rising they are happy to be in control of their money.

Interest Rate Spread

Remember that the Owe-it-Alls chose to borrow the entire $300,000 for their home—so they could invest the $300,000 they had into a "safe account," meaning an account where they could not lose their money. While they did not think they should pay cash for their house, they do wish to be conservative in the place they put their money securing their mortgage. They have other dollars in their Investment Tank but these dollars they feel should be in the Safe Tank with no chance of loss. Supposing the interest rate on their mortgage is 4%. What after tax rate of return would they need to earn on their investments to break even? On the surface, it looks like 4%, but it's actually only 3.1%, assuming they are in a 31% income tax bracket. Why? The mortgage interest deduction reduces the cost to borrow. They would only need to net around 3.1% after tax to be in control. They believe that 3.1% is well within their risk tolerance.

Key Concept: Net cost to borrow equals your loan rate less your tax bracket. If you receive a mortgage interest deduction, it reduces the investment risk you have to earn on your money for you to be in control.

Extra Principal Payments

Unlike the Free-n-Clears, the Pay-Extras did not have enough money to pay off their home up front. So they chose a shorter loan period and made extra principal payments to pay off their loan early. The 15-year loan requires more than a 30-year fixed payment creating the extra cash required.

Why did the Pay-Extras choose a 15-year mortgage? Survey says: The interest they think they will save. The key word is *think*. The perception is the shorter the loan, the lower the cost. But if that was true, then paying cash would make the most sense and it might if you do not calculate the opportunity cost on your money. We already looked at paying cash and found the Free-n-Clears would need to be able to sell their home in 30 years for $3,200,000 which may be possible but not probable.

The Pay-Extras may be surprised to learn that once they get their 15 year note paid off and start investing the 15 year payment amount, they will end up with the same amount they would have had had they invested the difference between the 15 and 30-year monthly mortgage payments for 30 years, assuming the same interest rate and tax bracket. On top of that they earned no interest on the money in the house and cut the time period in half for them to earn interest once they get their house paid off. Once their house is paid off, they can start saving but they have dramatically shortened the time available to earn compound interest. Compound interest works best over time and uninterrupted.

Key Concept: There is greater risk to earn any given rate of return over a shorter period than a longer period.

Tax Deductions

Perhaps one of the most overlooked aspects affecting mortgage decisions is the mortgage interest deduction.

Let's see how that impacts our couples.

Since the Free-n-Clears have no mortgage, they receive no deductions. However, with no mortgage payment, they had dollars available to maximize their contribution to a qualified retirement account at work, like a 401(k), which would qualify for an income tax reduction. When asked what was the main reason for their contribution to this account they said, "tax deductions." By contributing to their retirement plan, they deferred a tax to potentially pay their tax at a higher bracket later if tax rates increase, but they also gave up their known mortgage interest deduction today. The mortgage interest deduction is actually more valuable than the deduction on their 401(k) contribution deduction because of the fact that you know what the tax advantage is today but you do not know what tax rates will be in the future when you withdraw the 401(k) dollars. If you take a deduction today that is a lower tax rate than your tax rate when you withdraw the money, you lose.

The Pay-Extras received some deductions but their extra principal payments reduced their tax advantage with every extra payment. Unfortunately they also are likely to be putting money in their 401(k) or qualified plan at work to get a deduction while at the same time driving home to their house that they are paying off as fast as they can, killing the deduction they drove to work to get.

The Owe-it-Alls kept their money in a safe account, one where they could not lose. They have other monies invested at higher risk than those set aside to cover their mortgage. Although their mortgage rate was 4%, they only had to earn 3.1% after their tax deductions to cover their mortgage payments to the bank—giving them access and control of their money. They maximized their qualified plan deductions at work, enjoying the company match and maximized the mortgage interest deductions on their mortgage interest. They chose to have a mortgage loan and put their money to work knowing that if things ever got tight they had access to their money to help reduce financial stress.

You have heard several things that perhaps have challenged your thinking on this subject of a mortgage and as you can see, there is a lot to know.

As we said earlier, we believe you should have your house paid off. That said, this does not necessarily need to mean that one should not have a mortgage loan. What it means is that you need to have the money to be able pay off your mortgage. If you have a mortgage of $300,000 and you have $300,000 in a safe account, your house is "free and clear." Don't forget the house is an asset worth $300,000 as well. The big question is not should you have your house paid for, we agree you should.

The question is really who is going to control your money: you or the bank and mortgage market?

Having your home paid for is a safe financial position, but paid for without control may not be as safe as you once thought or it could be.

There is a form you need to become familiar with called the 1003b which is the Uniform Residential Mortgage Application. It is five pages long and is designed for the lending institutions to determine if you qualify for a mortgage loan.

Once you put your money in your house through "down payments" or "extra payments," you now must *qualify* to get it back. How does the thought of having to qualify to access *your* money sound? What it means is that you could be turned down. Let's look at what could cause that to happen.

Disability

So what would happen in the event of a disability to our couples?

The Free-n-Clears must complete the five pages of the 1003b mortgage application if they would like to access any of their money. In the event of a disability, what will the bank say? Most likely no, especially if they have limited sources of income. Disability from sickness or accident is the number one reason why people lose their homes in America.

The Pay-Extras would also be required to complete the 1003b form for the bank. Once again, the bank may still turn them down even though they have been making extra payments for years. They will still be required to make their full payment next month even if disabled to avoid foreclosure. Does that sound like a safe position to you?

The Owe-it-Alls, on the other hand, have complete control and access to their money. They can pay their mortgage payment with the interest they are earning on their money and should interest rates fall, they have access to the $300,000 principal in their account. They could pay their mortgage loan off anytime they wish but in the event of a disability, they did not want to experience the financial pressure of not having access to their capital.

All three should have personal disability policies for the maximum amount they can receive to cover potential income loss. Without it, they all may be forced to dip into their Savings and Investment Tanks which could be a problem.

Unemployment

What would happen if our couples lost their jobs? It would seem that if there was ever a time when one would need access to their money, it would be if they lost their job.

The Free-n-Clears must again fill out the form and the bank will most likely say "no" with no current income flowing into their model. They may hear, "when you get another job, call us." This can be a very stressful time when you are trying to sell a house and find employment at the same time. If they need to move to another state to find work, it can spell disaster if the mortgage market is not very good at the time for the seller.

If the Pay-Extras want to get some of the extra money they have put in the house while they look for a new job, they may be surprised at what they hear from the bank. Once again, the bank may be forced to say "no" until they can prove they have a solid source of income. What's worse, if they move to a new line of work, it may take two years before the bank will give them a decent look and if they give them a loan, it may not be at a competitive rate.

The Owe-it-Alls are still earning interest on their money and they have access to the account to withdraw what they need until they can get back on their feet, with no questions asked. Having access to their money will certainly reduce value of the tanks in which they have put putting money away for their future but having access to their money in the time of crisis can relieve a lot of stress.

Interest Rate Increase

What happens if mortgage interest rates increase and the couples need their money for a new car, medical emergency, or college education for their children?

The Free-n-Clears may be forced to refinance at a higher rate today to access their equity than the rate they could have secured earlier, plus they still must qualify to get the new loan, even though current interest rates are higher. When you need access to money, the lender is in the driver's seat. It would really hurt to borrow your own money at 8% to send you child to college knowing that you could have had the money at 4%.

The Pay-Extras are in the same boat as the Free-n-Clears.

The Owe-it-Alls have been in the driver's seat from day one and have complete access to their money and are not affected by rate increases because although they did not need to finance they financed for as long as possible. Should interest rates drop, they will be the first in line to refinance to the lower rate and another 30-year loan giving them even more time to maintain control and access of their money.

Interest Rate Decrease

What would happen to the couples if mortgage interest rates go down?

The Free-n-Clears will not even notice. They don't even hear the news that says mortgage interest rates have dropped to a historical low. They are blind to the opportunity.

The Pay-Extras may think about refinancing their remaining balance but that will cost them more money. With only a few years remaining on their 15-year loan, they may decide to just keep going on the road they are on. They probably would never even consider refinancing their current balance to a 30 year loan.

The Owe-it-Alls will want to refinance to a longer loan period to reduce their present payments, giving them more cash flow, increased control, and greater investment opportunities with even less risk if mortgage interest deductibility is still on the table. They will refinance their current 30-year loan for another 30 years to stretch out the time period, giving them the maximum interest deductions and even greater control.

Mortgage Payments during Retirement

The Free-n-Clears decided they did not want to make mortgage payments during retirement and their thinking was that if they had no mortgage payment, they would have more to spend. Rather than putting the money in their house, they could have had more money in their nest egg which could have paid their payments the rest of their life with money left over.

The money they have in their 401(k) will come out taxable and with no mortgage; they will not have offsetting mortgage interest deductions when they take their qualified plan distributions. A reverse mortgage may prove to be a good option, allowing them to get up to half of the home's value in tax free cash, leaving them with no monthly payments, should they need access to more capital.

The Pay-Extras were not thinking about retirement; they were concentrating on their current lifestyle. They could not pay their house off in full, so they chose the 15 year option. Like the Free-n-Clears, they will need to sell their house to access the equity or refinance to cash out equity which will put them in the same position as if they had a 30-year loan at the start. Once they retire, their potential to access the equity in their home by refinancing is diminished. They have the same reverse option available but if they have any balance on their loan, the reverse mortgage will pay off that loan first before providing tax free dollars.

The Owe-it-Alls will want to refinance before they leave employment to make qualification for a new 30 year loan easier. If they plan on moving, they will sell their home and can receive up to $500,000 of gain on their house tax free as a married couple ($250,000, if single). They will want to keep their cash at the closing, find a new home, put the least amount down and finance their retirement home as long as possible. If they decide to stay in their current house, they can do a reverse mortgage on the remaining equity to take a tax free withdraw. Remember their original $300,000 is still in their account compounding interest over the years.

One last thought. Many believe that leaving a house Free-n-Clear to their heirs is something to be desired. If you have more than one child, what do you think they are going to do with the house that you took such great pride to keep up and worked so hard to pay off? They are going to sell it and will probably not be as concerned as you would be to get the best price. They will most likely be more interested in getting it sold so they can move on with their life. If one wants the house the others will want the money. If the child that wants the house does not have the means to buy out the others it could cause bad blood between them.

Most likely, your children will not want to live in your house since they probably have their own homes and lives, perhaps even living in a different part of the country. Your house becomes a burden to keep up until it can be sold, not to mention getting all your stuff out so they can get it ready to sell. All your stuff is not going to fit into their house with all the stuff they have already and you will be surprised by how much of your stuff they throw away. So it's a good thing that you will know nothing about it.

Finally, by now you are probably looking at your house as a great place to sleep but not a great place for your money. It is a wonderful place to raise a family and enjoy having family and friends over for dinner, but it does not seem to be a great place for your money. In chapter 20, we will discuss other options available to put your money other than your house that are safer and provide more control with more benefits.

Let's review the quiz one more time.

True or False?

1. A large down payment will save you more money on your mortgage over time than a small down payment.
2. A 15-year mortgage will save more money over time than a 30-year mortgage.
3. Making extra principal payments saves you money.
4. The interest rate is the main factor in determining the cost of a mortgage.
5. You are more secure having your home paid off than financed one hundred percent.

The answers are all false.

Why?

Because during this conversation we've learned that, compared to the other couples, the Owe-it-Alls:

- are least affected by the impact of inflation,
- lose the least amount of money from down payments that earn zero interest,

- have more investment opportunities than the other couples,
- achieve the greatest return on the money they pay for their house,
- obtain the same appreciation on their home as the other couples,
- are able to maximize any interest rate spread,
- experience the least amount of loss from extra principal payments,
- receive the most tax deductions of any of the couples,
- maintain control of their money in the event of a disability,
- can still access their money in the event of unemployment,
- may be able to benefit from interest rate increases, and
- have the most opportunity to benefit from interest rate decreases.

Recommendations:

If your home mortgage is paid off, congratulations. Having a house that is paid for is not a problem, you should be commended, it is a great achievement. We would never recommend for you to refinance and cash out equity to invest in anything. A good question for you to think about is what are you doing now with the cash flow that was once required to make your mortgage payment? It would be wise to put those dollars to work for your future, rather than spending them on your current lifestyle if your future lifestyle is not fully funded.

Should you ever sell your house and need to buy another, perhaps this information will give you a different way to look at this subject.

Granted, there is a lot to know about a mortgage and this discussion is certainly not an exhaustive overview. What you don't know may be more important that what you do know. If your thinking was challenged about this subject, you should spend some time with the person who gave you this book or an advisor and look at your specific situation using your numbers. It is possible that more money will go through your mortgage than any other area in your financial life, including your retirement plan; so it makes sense to pay close attention to avoid unnecessary mistakes along the way. Your house is a major capital expense and how you go about paying for it is just one of the many financial decisions you will need to make to find the balance between your current lifestyle desires and your future lifestyle requirements.

Take the time to gain control of this important area of your financial life.

	Free-n-Clear	Pay-Extra	Owe-it-All
Impact of inflation	Largest loss	Some loss	**Least**
Down Payment	Largest loss	Some loss	**Least**
Investment Opportunities	Monthly	None	**Maximum**
Home as an investment	Least return	Some return	**Maximum return**
Appreciation	**Equal**	**Equal**	**Equal**
Interest Rate Spread	None	None	**Maximum**
Extra Principal Payments	Largest loss	Some loss	**Least**
Tax Deductions	None	Some	**Maximum**
Disability	Loss of access	Loss of access	**Control**
Unemployment	Loss of access	Loss of access	**Control**
Interest Rate Increase	No opportunity	No opportunity	**Opportunity**
Interest Rate Decrease	No opportunity	Some opportunity	**Most opportunity**

Chapter 16:
Taxes: Keep a Close Eye on Your Partner

Taxes certainly play a major role in your ability to accumulate money for your future and they have a direct impact on the dollars you have available today to spend on your current lifestyle. So it makes perfect sense that you constantly look at this area of your financial obligations making sure you are as efficient as you can be. Your federal income tax liability is no doubt your largest annual expense and will be your entire life.

You should take an active role in making sure that you are not paying more than required. Lack of understanding and due diligence in this area can lead to losing a great deal of money unnecessarily. A good CPA and/or tax attorney can play an important role in your financial future, especially if you own a business.

If you own a business, then your business will take up the lion share of the yellow or Investment Tank which will supply most of your earned income. Owning a business offers advantages both with your business income as well as benefits that can be used to increase your current and future lifestyles.

> **You should take an active role in making sure that you are not paying more than required. Lack of understanding and due diligence in this area can lead to losing a great deal of money unnecessarily.**

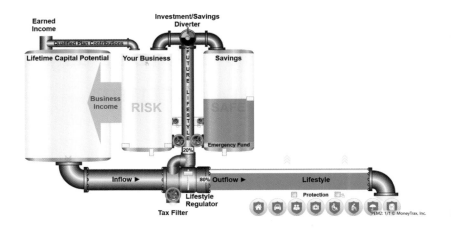

Federal Income tax is not the only thing that will need your constant attention. Many states also require state income taxes on your annual earnings to be paid on top of those dollars collected by the federal government. In addition to federal and state income taxes, you will pay property tax and sales taxes.

> **There are many investment opportunities that will also require taxes on the gains during the year they were earned. There are other accounts that allow your gains to be deferred to the time of withdrawal or when they are sold.**

As a boy, my grandfather would tell me the old adage, "a penny saved is a penny earned," and I am sure you have heard it. Today, we need to change that to "a hundred dollars saved is a hundred dollars earned," but being aware of what you are paying in taxes can help you avoid unnecessary loses.

There are many investment opportunities that will also require taxes on the gains during the year they were earned. There are other accounts that allow your gains to be deferred to the time of withdrawal or when they are sold.

The initial dollars used to make the investment have already gone through the Tax Filter and are not subject to additional taxes; however, the interest those accounts earn is taxable. Accounts that pay interest or dividends are subject to taxes on the gain during that same year. The opportunity cost needs to be calculated to determine the true return potential of the investment.

How you pay your tax is another thing to which you should pay close attention. When your account shows a gain or a profit, the profit is taxed as ordinary income or capital gains. Seeing your account value go up is always a good thing but few ever pay the tax by taking withdrawals from their account. This requires the tax due to come from current lifestyle which is often already stretched to the limit. The tax on gains can impact your cash flow, especially if your earnings are significant. Since most do not pay the taxes due on their gains from the same investment account it is easy to miss the real impact and amount of taxes that are being paid.

There are several strategies that can help you minimize your tax liability while still taking advantage of the gains in your investment accounts. Let's look at an illustration of $100,000 in a taxable account earning 5% over 20 years with a tax rate of 30%.

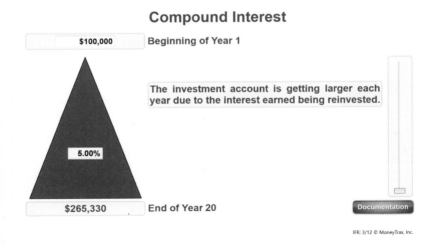

Compound Interest

| $100,000 | Beginning of Year 1 |

The investment account is getting larger each year due to the interest earned being reinvested.

5.00%

| $265,330 | End of Year 20 |

Documentation

IFR: 3/12 © MoneyTrax, Inc.

At the end of 20 years, the account value will be worth $265,330. Looks pretty good.

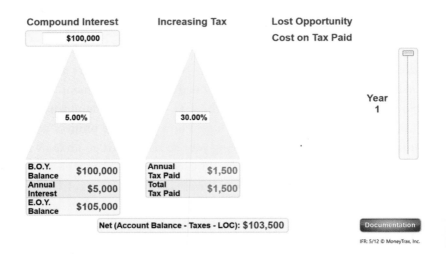

At the end of the first year, you would have earned $5,000 and you would be required to pay $1,500 in taxes on the gain for that year. Think again about how you are paying this tax. Are the tax dollars coming from draining money from the investment account or from your current lifestyle cash flow?

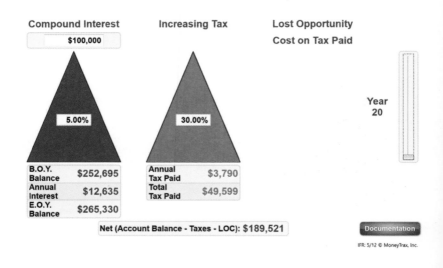

By the end of the 20th year, your account would be worth $265,330 and you would need to pay $3,790 in taxes in that year, with a total of taxes paid from your lifestyle over the period of $49,599. If you had paid the taxes due from the account your account balance would be $189,521.

The account value looks great because the taxes have been paid from your lifestyle, not the account. When the tax liability was small you may have been able to cover the taxes due without impacting your cash flow but as your account grows so does the tax which will have an even greater impact on your cash flow over time. But that is not the end of the story. Remember the term opportunity cost. If you pay a tax that you did not have to pay or could have avoided, you not only lost those dollars, but what those dollars could have earned had you been able to keep them.

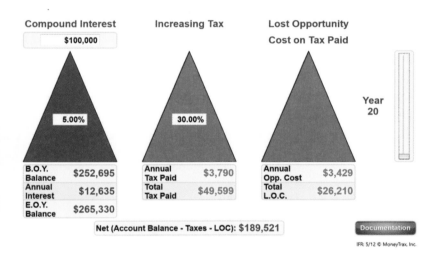

You will notice that you lost the $49,599 in taxes and an additional $26,210 in opportunity representing what the tax dollars would have earned in interest had you not had to pay them. If your money is earning 5% then you must also factor the cost of dollars lost at that same rate.

There are few rules from the federal government on taxable accounts compared to tax deferred accounts. Perhaps the fact that the federal government is your partner in these accounts may have something to do with it. Your partner, the government, did not use any of their money, did not take any risk in the investment, loses nothing if the investment fails and gets a huge share of the profits if you do well. Don't forget you had to stand in the tax line to pay taxes on the money you earned to make the investment and then had to get back in the same line again each year to pay taxes on the gains your investment earned.

If you are interested in keeping more of your money there are three strategies available to reduce your tax liability and increase the amount of money you get to keep.

The first strategy would be to move the interest earned to a tax favored account where it can grow tax deferred, thus flattening the tax due each year. By removing the earnings each year, the taxes due remain level or flat because the underlying account is not getting larger which creates the increase in taxes. Accounts earning a high rate of return are a good thing to have, but don't forget about the tax liability increasing when you roll the earnings back in the same account.

There are two options available on where to put your earnings after you have paid the tax. Depending on the type account you choose the earnings could grow either tax deferred, meaning you would the taxes later, or tax favored which would allow the earnings to grow tax deferred and come out tax free.

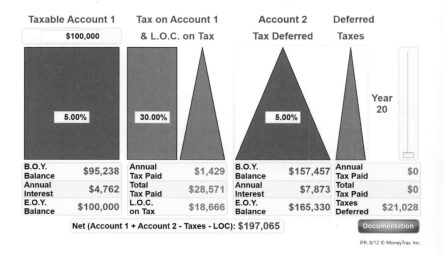

Should you decide to defer the taxes and pay them later your taxes would be $28,571 which leaves an account balance of $197,065.

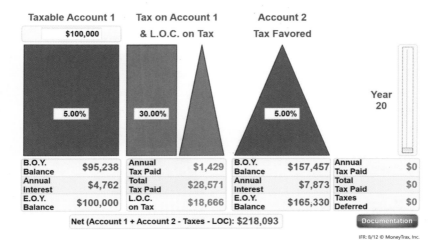

Taxable Account 1 $100,000	5.00%	Tax on Account 1 & L.O.C. on Tax	30.00%	Account 2 Tax Favored	5.00%	Year 20
B.O.Y. Balance	$95,238	Annual Tax Paid	$1,429	B.O.Y. Balance	$157,457	Annual Tax Paid	$0
Annual Interest	$4,762	Total Tax Paid	$28,571	Annual Interest	$7,873	Total Tax Paid	$0
E.O.Y. Balance	$100,000	L.O.C. on Tax	$18,666	E.O.Y. Balance	$165,330	Taxes Deferred	$0

Net (Account 1 + Account 2 - Taxes - LOC): $218,093

Documentation

IFR: 8/12 © MoneyTrax, Inc.

Note that by using the tax favored account your original investment account of $100,000 stays the same each year and your tax liability has been reduced from $49,599 to $28,093, saving you the difference with a balance of $218,093.

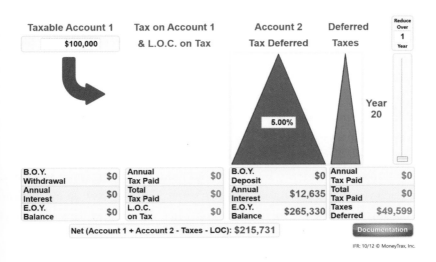

Taxable Account 1 $100,000	Tax on Account 1 & L.O.C. on Tax	Account 2 Tax Deferred	5.00%	Deferred Taxes	Reduce Over 1 Year	Year 20
B.O.Y. Withdrawal	$0	Annual Tax Paid	$0	B.O.Y. Deposit	$0	Annual Tax Paid	$0
Annual Interest	$0	Total Tax Paid	$0	Annual Interest	$12,635	Total Tax Paid	$0
E.O.Y. Balance	$0	L.O.C. on Tax	$0	E.O.Y. Balance	$265,330	Taxes Deferred	$49,599

Net (Account 1 + Account 2 - Taxes - LOC): $215,731

Documentation

IFR: 10/12 © MoneyTrax, Inc.

The above picture illustrates the results of the second strategy which would allow you to reduce your tax liability by moving your entire account at once from the taxable account to a tax deferred account. Taxes will not be due until you take the money, thus avoiding an opportunity cost lost.

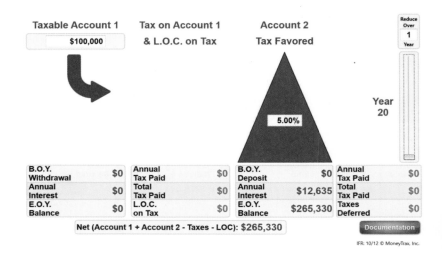

If you move the entire account to a tax favored position where there are no future taxes due, you would have $265,330, with no opportunity cost lost.

The third strategy would be to move principal and interest over a period of years rather than at once. This would allow you to reduce your tax liability slowly while still maintaining control of the account. While moving all the money from the taxable account at once may be more beneficial from a tax perspective you should also consider how doing so would impact your access to capital. Remember that accounts that promise higher returns or tax advantages often come with reduced access to your money. If accessibility is important then moving to a tax favored account over time may be your best choice.

The purpose for this discussion is for you to see you have other options besides leaving your money in a taxable account and paying more and more taxes each year as the account increases in value. Knowing how an investment is a taxed is fundamental to your decision when deciding which savings and investment accounts are right for you.

Remember that when you pay a tax that you could have avoided, you lost the opportunity of those dollars as well. Given a choice, deferring taxes is better than paying them annually and avoiding them where legally possible is best of all. The government is not going to make sure that you are minimizing your tax liability and if you overpay they will gladly take the money. Unfortunately, the tax system we have in place today is very complicated but the law suggests that you would be no less patriotic if you paid only the amount of tax required.

Chapter 17:
Qualified Plans: Pay Me Now or Pay Me Later

Your 401(k), IRA, SEP plan, and 403b reside in the investment tank specifically designed for your financial future. Your individual investment accounts are held inside qualified accounts which enable them to grow tax deferred until the time of distribution at which time they will be taxed. A qualified plan simply means that your contributions from your earned income are qualified by the federal government to go directly to the Investment Tank without first passing through the Tax Filter. In addition the money in the account is not subject to income tax on the growth until you take distribution of the funds. If you take constructive receipt of any of the money before age 59 ½, you must pay the taxes due at your tax rate at that time and a 10% penalty on the dollars withdrawn. You must begin distributions before at age 70 ½, or you will receive a 50% penalty on the RMD or required minimum distribution not taken.

> **A qualified plan simply means that your contributions from your earned income are qualified by the federal government to go directly to the Investment Tank without first passing through the Tax Filter.**

Keep in mind that these accounts were not designed to be the only place you have money for your retirement. In fact it is almost impossible to put away enough in these accounts to live like you live today and have your money last until your life expectancy. The fact that the amount of contributions allowed is limited suggests that you will need to put away more in other accounts than the government will allow you to put in qualified accounts.

While these accounts can be very effective in accumulating money for your financial future, especially if you get a matching contribution from your employer, one caution is the money in these accounts is not available before retirement age without tax and penalty. For many, restricted access may be seen as a good thing, since if they could get to the money, they would perhaps spend it and have little or nothing left in the account by the time they retire. This could be the primary reason the government imposes stiff penalties for early withdrawal.

On the other hand, it can create a great deal of financial stress during the accumulation years because of the lack of access to dollars in these accounts. You can have thousands of dollars in these accounts but it will do you little good in managing the day-to-day pressures of your current lifestyle since you can't get to the money without penalties. Lack of access to capital in these accounts can can give rise to one using credit cards for current lifestyle expenses, and ending up actually paying more interest to the credit card companies than they may be earning in their qualified retirement account. It would make little sense to pay interest on borrowed money to support your current lifestyle and at the same time, earn less interest on the money you are putting away for your future; however, this is a common occurrence for many. Imagine earning 6% on money in your 401k and paying 12%-21% interest on credit card purchases with after tax dollars.

Since your contribution to these accounts are usually taken out of your check before you get it be careful not to forget that the money in your qualified plan must one day pass through the Tax Filter. At that time your partner with take their share first and you will have the value of the withdrawal minus your tax rate at the time of withdrawal. These are not tax savings plans but tax deferred savings plans. It is important that you understand what is going on in your entire economic model and know how each area affects the others. This is another issue where balance plays an important role in your financial decisions.

Let's take a clearer picture of your qualified retirement dollars. Suppose you have $300,000 in the Investment Tank in qualified money. When you look at your account, you see this picture.

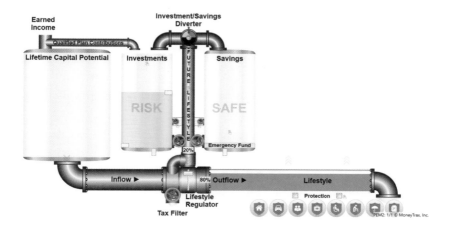

You get your statement and it shows that you have $300,000. This is how you see your account, but it is not an accurate picture. Now, take a look at this picture.

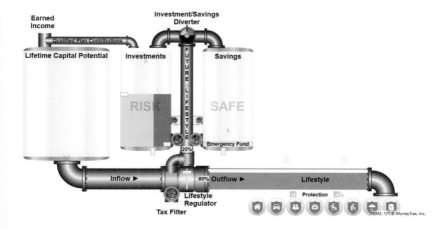

This picture is more accurate. The red stands for the taxes that you will owe when you take distributions at retirement. It represents the government's share of the account. Notice that their share comes out first. All the money in the tank is not yours. Remember that you have a partner in this account. The government did not say you don't owe any taxes when you put your money in your qualified plan, they said there are no taxes due now and you can pay us later. What will your tax rate be when you take the money out of your account? Now that is a good question and the following picture will illustrate the point.

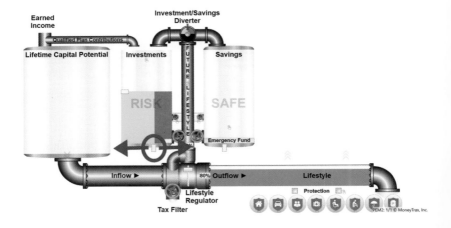

Notice that the slider just below the investment tank. The government controls this slider and can move it as they wish. If they raise taxes, your value will be less; if they lower taxes, your value will be more.

Let me tell you a story to help you better understand. Suppose you asked me to loan you $10,000 dollars and I handed you a check for that amount. Before you took the check, you would ask me two questions. The first would be what is the interest rate that will be charged on the loan and the second is when do you have to pay it back or what is the length of terms on the loan. Suppose I said, "you know I have plenty of money right now and do not need any payments at this time. However there will come a time when I will need the money and when I know how much I need, I can then calculate how much interest to charge you to get how much I need, we will work the payment out later…" Would you cash that check?

Probably not, and this is not to say that putting money in a qualified plan is a bad thing but rather this is how it works. As long as you understand how it works, you can determine if it is right for you. If taxes are lower when you take the money than they were when you put it in, you will have more. If taxes are higher, you will have less. Not making the right decision can cause you to lose a great deal of money over your working career. There is more to be had in avoiding the losses than the winners.

Many people ask, how can I know what tax rate I will be in when I retire? Two things to consider that can help you answer that question. The first is, are you a saver? The second question is, are you saving enough to retire in the future at the same income level you enjoy today adjusted for inflation? Unfortunately, many Americans are not savers and many of those who do save may not be saving enough.

If you are not saving enough, it is quite probable you could be in a lower tax bracket in the future with less income available. Many are of the misconception that they will need less money in retirement than they do while they are working. This may give you a different way to see the problem.

Suppose you are going to retire at age 65 and you are going to now live off the dollars you have put away in your tanks. Let's assume you are married and you each can get by on $10 dollars a meal until your life expectancy at age 90. That's three meals a day at $10 each times two, or $60 dollars a day just to eat. 365 days a year times 25 years is 18,250 meals to feed both of you. $60 a day times 365 day a year for 25 years is $547,500. OK you don't think it will cost you $10 a meal in the future. Suppose you could pay $5.00 a meal it would be $273,750 just to eat. How much did you say you would have in your tanks when you retire?

If you are a saver and putting away enough to secure your future, you need to determine if you believe taxes will be higher or lower when you withdraw your money from your qualified account. Going back to the history of taxes can give you some insight into this decision. The average since they started taking taxes in 1913 is 58.06%. With a government that is twenty trillion in debt and the power to set the tax rate as desired, you should take a pause to determine if tax deferred qualified plans are a good choice for you or not.

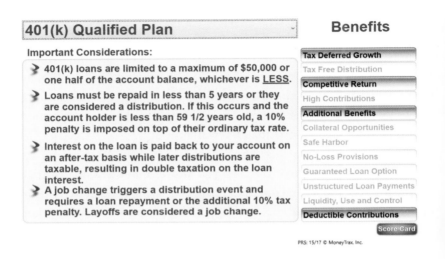

PRS: 15/17 © MoneyTrax, Inc.

As you can see, qualified plans do offer the benefit of your money growing tax deferred and the potential for a competitive return. It may provide additional benefits like loan provisions to allow you to borrow up to 50% of the accounts value to a maximum of $50,000. Perhaps the largest perceived benefit is the ability to deduct contributions to these plans. As we discussed earlier, that benefit may be seen differently by those who retire in a higher tax bracket than they were in during their accumulation years. In addition to the benefits, one should also be aware of other considerations as listed in the picture above.

The greatest benefit of making contributions to a qualified plan is that of the company match on the dollars you put in the plan but not all companies offer this benefit. Obviously any match from your employer is better than no match at all and if you get a match you should put in as much as you can up to the matching amount. If you do not receive a match, the benefit is your money can grow tax deferred until distribution which beats putting money in a taxable account every time. Contributions above the match receive the benefit of a tax deduction but offer no access during the years of accumulation which can be an issue. If you carry a credit card balance and make contributions above the match, the interest you are losing may be higher than the interest you are earning which could be zeroing out the purpose of your non-matched contribution.

If you get no match and you have credit card debt you may consider stopping contributions until you get that problem under control. Putting dollars in your left pocket to earn 5 or 6%, while paying 12-21% on credit card interest in your right pocket, does not seem prudent. You can always start making contributions to your qualified account again when you have your finances under control.

The match will be a great help in the future because the matching dollars may pay some or all of your tax liability. If you put in a dollar and the company matches 50% on that dollar and you are in a 33% tax bracket at the time of withdrawal, the match covered your taxes due and you get your dollar back at interest. The contributions over and above the match offer tax postponement but the benefit, if any, on those dollars will depend on the tax rate at the time of withdrawal and what the rate was when the contribution was made. You will not know if this was a good idea or not until you can compare your withdrawal tax rate to the tax rate you had at the time of your contribution.

If you don't get a matching contribution, you should think hard about tying up your money till age 59 1/2 with no access simply for the opportunity to postpone your taxes until later.

Non-Qualified Money:

Other investments in the investment tank are considered non-qualified, meaning they do not qualify for tax-deferral on the growth earned in the account and the underlying investment must be made with after tax dollars rather than pretax dollars. Since the original investment dollars are made with after tax dollars, there is no tax required on distributions of those dollars since taxes were paid on them earlier; however, there is tax due on the gains received from the growth while in the account. Currently, gains can be taxed as ordinary income or capital gains depending on the underlying investment and must be paid each year the account shows a profit.

As we discussed in our last chapter on taxes it is important to understand that any gains in non-qualified accounts will be taxed annually and few investors ever withdraw money from these accounts to help them offset the increased tax liability created from the interest earned. Rather than reducing the account value, the taxes are most often paid from one's current lifestyle and as their account increases, current lifestyle decreases. This problem is difficult to see until the account grows to such an amount that the taxes cannot be ignored any longer. This may not cause significant cash flow issues in the early days of the investment account but over time as the value of the account increases, so do the annual taxes which when paid from lifestyle, can put stress on current lifestyle cash flow.

Tax deferral is always better than taxable because it avoids the opportunity cost loss on taxes were paid which could have been avoided. If you lose a dollar that you did not have to lose you not only lost that dollar but what the dollar could have earned for you had you been able to keep it.

Chapter 18: College: Your kids are ready, are you?

Remember what you learned in chapter 14—you finance everything you buy and sending your kids to college is no exception.

You either lose the opportunity to earn interest by paying cash and draining a tank to pay for this lifestyle expense or pay interest to another institution for the privilege of using their money, paying it back off over time. What's the problem with draining an asset to pay for a current lifestyle expense? You kill compounding.

Parents tend to view college as an investment instead of a lifestyle choice or expense. You are making a huge investment in the lives of your children but it is an expense for you. None of the money you spend on your children's education will return to you. How you pay for this expense called education can unknowingly and unnecessarily interrupt compounding, giving away valuable dollars from interest lost that could prove vital to your future lifestyle during retirement. You create loss by removing money from your current Savings and Investment Tanks to pay for college-related expenses or you suspend contributions to your future tanks during the college years, which also kills compounding.

The big question is how are you going to pay for college? If you pay cash, you self-finance. Your intention is to pay yourself back by putting the money back with monthly cash flow. While this seems to make sense on one level, the reality is that few ever do get around to putting the money back and even fewer put back the interest the account lost while their money was out.

The most effective way to manage your Personal Economic Model is to make sure you "don't cross the red line," meaning that you don't drain a tank or an asset designated for your future to pay for a current lifestyle expense. It is much safer and less stressful for you to maintain control of your money and finance your standard of living than it is to drain a tank that is earning interest.

The reality is that you are responsible for your financial future and you may or may not feel obligated to pay for your child's college education. If you are going to pay for college, you will want to know the most efficient way to do it.

If you have not been paying attention to the cost of a college education, this graph will be an eye opener.

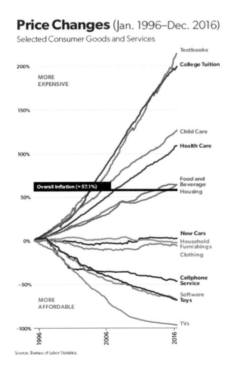

Price Changes (Jan. 1996–Dec. 2016)
Selected Consumer Goods and Services

Source: Bureau of Labor Statistics.

It is important that you and your student discuss the total cost early in your college search. Your college-bound student needs to fully understand the economic impact this expense will have on your retirement as well as other children in the family who will require the same or more capital. Should they go to a state university or private college? State schools tend to require five years rather than four to get the proper classes to complete graduation requirements. Private schools could work ou to be less expensive than state schools, offering more money to students they consider attractive, especially if they can graduate in four years rather than five.

Without a clear direction from your student of what they want to do with the degree they are going to get, you can most likely count on paying too much to send them. College is a very expensive place to decide what you want to be and what you want to do and unfortunately, many finish without every knowing.

Parents unknowingly and unnecessarily wreak havoc on their future when it comes to paying for college for two primary reasons:

Furniture, clothes and cars take as much of our monthly paycheck as they did 20 years ago.

TVs, cell phones and toys cost us less.

College, on the other hand, costs exponentially more. We simply can't approach paying for our children's education the way our parents approached funding our college experience.

College costs double every decade and triple in the 17 years from birth to college enrollment.

Most parents can't pay for a year of college out of monthly cash flow – let alone 4 or 5 years. So financing a substantial portion of the cost is a strategy that is a must. Understanding the financing options you have available and the need to focus on cash flow vs. assets to fund this expense is critical to creating the best possible outcome for you today as well as your future.

1. They think of college as an investment, not a major lifestyle expense, and
2. They wait too long to start planning for this six-figure expense.

"One action many families aren't undertaking, however, is developing a plan to pay for college. Even though nine in 10 surveyed said they anticipated college attendance since their child was in pre-school, less than half (42%) said they made a plan to pay for it."
- 2017 How America Saves for College, Sallie Mae's 10th National Study of College Students and Parents

The most recent Sallie Mae study tells us that students themselves are paying for 30% of their college expenses through working, savings, and loans while parents are shelling out another 31% of the total cost of college through income, savings, and loans. The rest of the money is OPM – other people's money. That includes federal and state financial aid, scholarships and grants from the colleges themselves, third party scholarships, and gifts from relatives or friends.

The fact is that this approach is not working. Student loan default rates are at all-time highs and parents are finding themselves having to work 10+ years longer before retiring to make up for the dollars lost from draining one of their Investment and Savings Tanks to cover college.

Paying for college is like buying a new car annually, and giving the car away at the end of the every year your child is enrolled in college. If you have more than one child, you are in for a long and expensive ride.

So let's compare buying a car to buying a year of college from a financial perspective. In Chapter 14 we learned that the cost to pay cash for a $30,000 car costs exactly the same as financing it over time at the same interest rate. We came to the conclusion that financing using OPM and maintaining control of our money, rather than paying cash and self-financing and giving up control, was a better option. We also learned that killing compounding was a terrible option because compound interest works best over time, uninterrupted and draining a tank means we not only lost the money, but the interest it could have earned had we been able to keep it.

The same principal is true when it comes to paying for college. You finance everything you buy and if you pay cash, you are self-financing. In Chapter 20 on the private reserve, we will discuss in more detail your financing options and how to keep your money earning interest without having to drain the tank.

This is where most mistakes are made. You surrender an existing asset that is earning interest to pay for college, so you don't have to borrow and pay interest. When you surrendered the asset, you lost not only the interest it would have earned, but you also lost control of that money. Not having access to money while your kid is in school is not exactly a recipe for stress-free living.

Suppose you had an investment account that was earning exactly the same interest as the interest you would owe if you financed your child's education using student loans. Would you feel more comfortable cashing in your investment and giving the college the lump sum and then begin saving to put back all the money you took out? Or would you feel safer keeping your money and using the interest you are earning to help you cover the college expense, maintaining liquidity, use, and control of your money? Remember, paying cash does not make it cost less.

The savings plan often suggested for college is a 529 or Coverdell Education Savings Account (ESA). Your aftertax contributions are most often invested in the yellow tank, meaning your money is at risk. Your money grows tax deferred and when it is time for college, the money comes out tax free but you must now drain the tank, giving up the interest you were once earning. Money in these accounts does not compound interest – it appreciates or depreciates, according to the market. If you do not use this money for qualified education expenses, you are taxed on the gain and incur a 10% penalty.

Those are the good things about the 529. Perhaps the worst thing is that you have to drain the tank and throw the tank away. What if you could put away aftertax dollars in an account that you could use for any purpose with not restrictions on what you use the money for and no penalties? What if you could borrow against the tank rather than from it and keep your money compounding and keep making contributions to the tank even when your kid is out of college? What you don't know could cost you.

College is a very expensive lifestyle choice. Before choosing which college, you and your child need to adopt a consumer purchase mentality based on how much money you have available to cover the cost. Can you really afford to buy a new car every five years and throw it away and still have enough money for you to retire?

You can't afford to spend everything you have put away for your future retirement because little Johnny wants to go across the country to a school that costs twice as much as other institutions, and takes five and not four years to get a degree in basket weaving only to then live on his own in an apartment off campus, driving a new car. Don't forget about an allowance!

You are sending them to college to get an education and their education in reality perhaps should be their first lesson. Reality is a tough thing and it is probably time your teenager got their first dose if they have not caught on already.

There are a few important questions you and your teen need to work on together to determine which school is right for them and you.

How much will we need to start and how much will it take to finish?

Where are the best places for me to put my money until college begins?

What sources are available to help me pay for the cost?

Let's tackle these one at a time…

How much will we need to start and how much to finish?

It may help you to know that few parents have enough money put away in a college fund account to cover their student's entire college experience. Most are going to have to do some creative financing to get the job done. Position A would be being able to send your kids to college without putting any money down, using free grants and scholarships if available, and financing the balance using loans.

	In-State U	Out-of-State U	Private U	Elite U
4 Year Cost of Attendance	$100,000	$192,000	$220,000	$275,000
10%	$10,000	$19,200	$22,000	$27,500
20%	$20,000	$38,400	$44,000	$55,000

Where are the best places to put money until we need it?

Where you have your money does affect access to student loans and scholarships. Most parents don't realize how you answer this question is critical. It turns out that where you save money for college can significantly impact how much you will have to pay and your financing options.

The financial aid formulas pay particular attention to a few categories of assets:

	FAFSA	CSS Profile
Cash (savings, checking, money market)	X	X
Savings Bond	X	X
Investments (529s, Coverdell ESAs, mutual funds, ETFs, stocks & bonds, UTMA/UGMAs)	X	X
Annuities (non-qualified contracts only – meaning not registered as an IRA)		X
Life Insurance (cash value)		
Retirement Accounts (IRAs, 401ks, 403b, 457, etc.)		
Home Equity		X

X = included in the calculation for financial aid purposes

Few parents are aware of the fact that certain savings vehicles – the ones marked with an X - will reduce the amount of financial aid they are eligible to receive by 5.64%. The amount of money you have currently and your ability to pay (your current income) is weighed against your EFC or the Expected Family Contribution towards the cost of college. Following is a quick reference guide to give you some indication on what you will be expected to pay.

QUICK REFERENCE GUIDE

2017-2018 Federal EFC Quick Reference Table

	Number of Dependent children			
AGI	1	2	3	4
$30,000	$998	$0	$0	$0
$32,500	$1,435	$582	$0	$0
$35,000	$1,871	$1,018	$0	$0
$37,500	$2,307	$1,455	$666	$0
$40,000	$2,733	$1,891	$1,103	$0
$42,500	$3,142	$2,328	$1,539	$625
$45,000	$3,074	$2,739	$1,975	$1,061
$47,500	$3,539	$3,148	$2,399	$1,498
$50,000	$4,004	$3,081	$2,808	$1,934
$52,500	$4,412	$3,545	$3,217	$2,343
$55,000	$4,951	$4,010	$3,159	$2,752
$57,500	$5,383	$4,419	$3,624	$3,161
$60,000	$6,015	$4,958	$3,972	$3,096
$62,500	$6,500	$5,391	$4,511	$3,560
$65,000	$7,244	$6,023	$5,050	$4,025
$67,500	$7,834	$6,510	$5,499	$4,437
$70,000	$8,708	$7,253	$6,131	$4,976
$72,500	$9,581	$7,846	$6,636	$5,412
$75,000	$10,455	$8,719	$7,380	$6,044
$80,000	$12,202	$10,466	$8,867	$7,277
$85,000	$13,949	$12,214	$10,615	$8,747
$90,000	$15,697	$13,961	$12,362	$10,495
$95,000	$17,219	$15,655	$14,109	$12,242
$100,000	$18,731	$17,168	$15,740	$13,989
$105,000	$20,244	$18,680	$17,252	$15,557
$110,000	$21,756	$20,192	$18,764	$17,069
$115,000	$23,268	$21,587	$20,159	$18,464
$120,000	$24,016	$22,218	$20,790	$19,095

2017-2018 Federal EFC Quick Reference Table

	Number of Dependent Children			
AGI	1	2	3	4
$125,000	$25,677	$24,165	$22,330	$20,635
$130,000	$27,335	$25,301	$23,874	$22,175
$135,000	$28,993	$26,959	$25,414	$23,719
$140,000	$30,651	$28,617	$26,954	$25,259
$145,000	$32,309	$30,275	$28,495	$26,800
$150,000	$33,967	$31,933	$30,035	$28,340
$155,000	$35,578	$33,544	$31,646	$29,833
$160,000	$37,180	$35,155	$33,257	$31,327
$165,000	$38,721	$36,738	$34,868	$32,760
$170,000	$40,261	$38,279	$36,432	$34,077
$175,000	$41,802	$39,819	$37,973	$35,512
$180,000	$43,342	$41,359	$39,513	$36,947
$185,000	$44,882	$42,900	$40,976	$38,381
$190,000	$46,423	$44,440	$42,410	$39,816
$195,000	$48,010	$46,028	$43,892	$41,298
$200,000	$49,598	$47,615	$45,374	$42,779
$205,000	$51,185	$49,182	$46,855	$44,261
$210,000	$52,772	$50,664	$48,337	$45,743
$215,000	$54,360	$52,145	$49,819	$47,224
$220,000	$55,947	$53,627	$51,300	$48,706
$225,000	$57,535	$55,109	$52,782	$50,188
$230,000	$59,015	$56,552	$54,226	$51,631
$235,000	$60,438	$57,975	$55,649	$53,054
$240,000	$61,861	$59,398	$57,072	$54,477
$245,000	$63,284	$60,821	$58,494	$55,900
$250,000	$64,707	$62,244	$59,917	$57,323
$275,000	$71,821	$69,359	$67,032	$64,438

NEED-BASED AID ELIGIBILITY at 2 yr public, 4 yr public, 4 yr private, elite 4 yr colleges

NEED-BASED AID ELIGIBILITY at 4 yr public, 4 yr private and elite 4 yr colleges

NEED-BASED AID ELIGIBILITY at 4 yr private and elite 4 yr colleges

NEED-BASED AID ELIGIBILITY at elite 4 yr colleges

NO NEED-BASED AID ELIGIBILITY

It would be poor planning if you started saving early for college, took risk, and the place where you saved your money reduced the amount of financial aid which could have qualified to receive by 5.64%.

Few also fail to understand the costs, distribution limitations, or tax consequences of the various accounts available for their savings dollars. Here are several account options you should consider when saving for college, comparing the benefits provided by each. Accounts with the highest potential rate of return should not be your primary objective.

What sources are available to help me pay for the cost?

When it comes to paying for college, there are actually three areas for you to consider: free money, found money and borrowed money.

1: Is there any opportunity for my student to receive free money?
You should explore every option available to get free financial help first.

2: There may be inefficiencies were you could potentially be losing dollars unnecessarily that could help you with the cost by freeing up cash flow?

Found Money

A big one is how you are paying for your mortgage. Putting extra money on your mortgage loan can create a huge problem, when it comes to future access to capital. The number one place parents go to help them with college expenses is the equity in their home. Make sure you review the chapter on mortgages and fully understand the role your mortgage loan plays in your financial future. The money you put in your house does not earn interest and you may be turned down or limited to what you can borrow against your house when college rolls around. Over paying your taxes is a problem as well.

You should be looking to be as efficient as you can when it comes to paying your taxes because if you overpay, the government is not going to send any money back to you. The tax law say you are required to pay what you owe and no more. There is a difference between tax evasion and tax avoidance. It's five years in the federal penitentiary. We don't want you in prison while your child is in college. Compounding interest in taxable accounts creates an increased tax liability and create a tax which could be avoided by moving the money to a more tax efficient account.

If you are over funding your qualified plan contributions for your retirement and you are going to be short when it comes to paying for college, you may want to consider doing up to the company match and no more. The only benefit of dollars above the match is your taxes will be postponed until you take the money. If you have to access this money before at age 59 ½, you are going to pay a 10% penalty. Knowing the rules can keep you from transferring money away unnecessarily.

Finally, how you pay for major capital purchases can cause stress down the road. Major purchases are anything you can't afford to pay for in full with monthly cash flow. By being more efficient and effective on how you pay for your house, reducing and minimizing your taxes, how and where you save for retirement and how you pay for major capital purchases—the biggest being how you are going to pay for college—you can redirect those lost dollars to help you pay for college without you having to drain a tank or reduce your present standard of living.

Most importantly, money you could be losing unnecessarily may allow you to continue to feed your future lifestyle (contributing to the yellow and green tanks) while meeting the cash flow challenges of the lifestyle expense called college. The difference between success and failure during the critical college years boils down to understanding that college is a cash flow challenge, not a savings challenge.

3: What are all my finance options? List every option you have available to borrow using other people's money rather than yours to finance the cost over time allowing you to use current lifestyle dollars rather than future lifestyle dollars. Potential options may include:
    student loans,
    home equity line of credit,
    refinance to a 30-year loan to free up cash flow,
    401(k) loan,
    collateralize an account that is earning you more interest than the loan, or borrow from a parent or grandparent,

Once you have identified all your options, you can then begin to determine which option works best for you.
1. Which option offers the best interest rate?

2. Which option offers the best repayment option that will fit my cash flow?
3. Which option will allow me to maintain control of my principal and make monthly payments?

A recipe for success in most households would look something like this:

Free $	Found $	Borrowed $
30% - 50%	20% - 40%	50% - 70%
Other People's Money	Current Cash Flow	Future Cash Flow
College scholarships & grants, Need-based financial aid, Regional reciprocity discounts, ROTC programs, 3rd party scholarships	Money you could be losing unknowingly and unnecessarily from cash flow inefficiencies.	Stafford student loans, Parent Plus loans, Home Equity Line of Credit, PLI collateralized loan

You should sit down with an advisor who specializes in college planning who can help you put together a workable plan. You should find an advisor that is knowledgeable about how to help you find free money, found money or borrowed money. Up to 80% of college financing requires qualification for free and borrowed funds: academically (GPA, test scores), athletically/artistically (performance), financially (income and assets) or medically (life insurance). If you are not maximizing your opportunities in all three, you are overpaying.

More often than not, it's the unique combination of these factors that ultimately determines your ability to pay for college with the least out-of-pocket cost. Every household can create a better recipe for success when it comes to funding for college but you need to take advantage of every option available to be as efficient and effective as possible. What you don't know can result in thousands of dollars lost unnecessarily.

Said another way, you can create a reasonable game plan for sending your child to college while exiting the labor and delivery room, but it won't come into sharp focus until their junior year of high school, when you know what kind of student you're planning for and can identify the schools that can best meet their needs academically, socially, and financially. Too many families apply to colleges without knowing where they stand in terms of free and borrowed money, resulting in overpaying.

If you plan ahead, you can get a plane ticket at a reasonable price. If you wait till the week you want to travel to purchase, you are going to pay more. Planning for how you are going to pay for your child's education is no different. Starting to plan today and finding an advisor who specializes in college funding can save you thousands and save you from a very stressful situation if you don't.

Case Study:

Paul is the proud father of three kids, and he and his wife, Janice, live well within their means. Paul recently assumed responsibility for his father's business and enlisted Janice's help to run the day-to-day operations. They take home about $80,000 a year but have managed to save some money for retirement. They have almost $90,000 in three Uniform Transfer to Minors Act (UTMA) accounts for their kids. Paul firmly believes that "college isn't optional in my household."

Paul and Janice had three financial goals in mind:
1. get the kids through college with little or no student loan debt,
2. make significant and consistent contributions to their retirement accounts
3. pay down their mortgage as quickly as possible.

Little did they know that saving money for their kids in the UTMA accounts actually drove their EFC higher and limited their financial aid eligibility. In other words being responsible and saving for their childrens' education counts against them when it comes to need-based financing.

Because UTMA accounts are considered the students' assets (children assume control of UTMA accounts at age eighteen in most states), the financial aid formulas assess those assets more heavily.

The financial aid formulas assume that if students have money in their name, those funds most certainly should be used for college. The result is that the financing options are limited because of where the parents saved money for college.

Paul and Janice worked with an advisor that is knowledgeable about free, found, and borrowed money for college. They moved the UTMA money to accounts that are "financial aid invisible." This strategic choice reduced the family's expected contribution (EFC) between 18%-48% (depending on the school's individual formula) and increased their aid eligibility by $130,000 over the nine years their kids would be in college.

With the kids' money gone from the family balance sheet for financial aid reporting purposes, they can use more of other people's money for college and direct their savings toward retirement.

When you are looking to buy a car, the car salesperson is anxious to get you behind the wheel for a test drive because they are appealing to your emotions—how the car handles and smells and how you feel while driving it. Once you visualize parking the car in your garage, the sale is over. When you decide to make the purchase, a salesperson will get creative and find a way to help you pay for it.

Colleges do the same thing, appealing to the emotions of an eighteen year-old who wants to say they are going to their favorite school and letting their parents brag that their child has been accepted is a great time in the life of any family.

But emotions are not good stewards of your capital and you need to make sure you understand what you're signing up for before applying to college.

Using the Personal Economic Model to guide you toward a plan that uses all three types of money for college is the best way to make sure you never cross the red line. Don't pay for current lifestyle expenses with future lifestyle assets. Spend time searching for money you could be losing unknowingly and unnecessarily to help you with the cash flow you will need to finance this major capital purchase called college. Collateralize your assets if you must but do not give up control by draining a tank. Finance the college expense as you would any other major capital purchases and keep feeding your tanks to solidify your financial future while you are helping your child begin theirs.

Special thanks to Beth Walker:

I would like to give special thanks to a good friend and nationally recognized college planning advisor Beth Walker for her contribution to this chapter. She is the founder of the Center for College Solutions and has written a book titled "Never Pay Retail For College". College planning requires specialized knowledge to navigate the best way to pay for this major capital expense. You should consult a qualified professional to maximize your opportunities and minimize your expense.

Chapter 19:
Major Capital Purchases: "Anything You Can't Pay for in Full with Monthly Cash Flow"

A major capital purchase is anything that you can't pay for in full with monthly cash flow. Life is full of these types of expenses, some we know are coming but most just happen without any warning. They can be as small as paying for a new set of tires or as big as paying for your daughter's wedding or your son's college. How we handle these financial costs can make or break us.

Paying cash is financing—it is self-financing. How we finance these major capital purchases is very important. The very fact that you can't pay for the expense with monthly cash flow requires you to come up with a plan to finance it. Will you self-finance using your own money by draining one of your Savings or Investment Tanks or will you finance using OPM (other people's money) and pay for it over time with your current lifestyle cash flow? Being able to finance an expense over time gives one an opportunity to reduce the immediate pressure imposed and attack it over time. Some MCPs (major capital purchases) need only a few months' relief to solve, others can take years.

We have discussed that if you can help it, you never want to drain a future Savings or Investment Tank using a future lifestyle asset to pay for a current lifestyle expense. We recommend you keep money in your tanks compounding interest uninterrupted, allowing for your future lifestyle monies to keep moving you forward while you pay over time for major capital expenses from your current lifestyle cash flow.

Halting contributions to your savings and investment accounts until you get major expenses out of the way puts even more pressure on your financial future by reducing the time available to solve your future lifestyle cash flow requirements. The problem with major capital purchases is that you can't always see them coming to prepare. You finally get one expense behind you but you can be certain there will be others to follow.

The opportunity to pay for these expenses over time by financing them using OPM allows you to continue making contributions towards your financial future, continually moving you forward financially and still have enough to cover the expense using your current lifestyle monthly cash flow. Feed your tanks, finance your lifestyle.

We learned in the chapter on mortgages that your house, perhaps your largest major capital purchase, costs the same if you pay cash or you finance, assuming you can earn the same interest rate on your investments as the loan rate. If you want to get it paid off earlier, put your extra money in your tank where you are earning interest and you control your money rather than the bank. The same principal holds true for every major capital purchase. Paying extra on the loan does not make it cost less. You must give up extra cash flow today to pay a loan off early. You could have just as easily put the extra dollars in your tank and earned the same amount of interest you hoped to avoid paying. Giving up control of your money today to have extra cash flow tomorrow does not put you in a safer financial position. Guard your collateral capacity and finance your lifestyle.

If for some reason you just can't get this strategy, at least put your money in your tank until you get enough to drain the tank by writing one check to pay off your loan in full. You would not have to give up control of your money until you have enough to pay off your loan. You will be surprised to see how difficult it is to write a lump sum check and give up control versus keeping your money and writing checks with smaller monthly payments. Once you have the money, you don't want to give it away. Access to capital is a tremendous stress reliever.

Some capital purchases you will be able to finance without using your money as collateral. A car is a perfect example. You can make the purchase with just your signature using the car as collateral, not your money. It is important not to drain a tank for a current lifestyle expense and you should equally protect giving up your collateral. Having money is not the same as having collateral. You may be worth a lot on paper but the amount of money you can get your hands on in times of financial trouble is something altogether different. Guard your collateral capacity.

Remember, transportation is a current lifestyle expense. Paying for the car faster will not make it cost any less and maybe even more, if you can earn more on your money than you have to pay to use someone else's. Paying your car off faster does not improve your future financial position but does free up cash flow. Does it make sense to pay extra on your car note today to can get the loan paid off so you can have extra cash flow later? The temptation once the note is paid off is to spend the additional cash flow, not save it, once payments have stopped. Saving the additional cash flow once the note is paid in full is a rare occurrence and one rarely pays themselves back the interest they could have earned had they put the extra money in their tank. Self-financing takes extreme discipline.

Draining an asset for a current lifestyle expense should be your last resort. If you put the money back as well as the interest you would have earned, you did no harm but keep in mind that human nature is working against you. When you borrow from yourself by draining one of your future lifestyle tanks, you have no payments and no pressure today to return the money. The pressure did not go away because you paid cash for your purchase. If you don't put the money back plus the interest lost the pressure will return much stronger when you do not have the money to cover your future lifestyle requirements.

From time to time, there will be other major capital purchases that may require you to provide collateral to secure financing. Keep in mind that when you use your collateral you are reducing your access to that amount of capital until the lien has been removed. Position A would always be to borrow against your money, preferably at a lower interest rate than you are earning if that is an option rather than draining a tank and killing compounding on the amount borrowed.

When financing using OPM there may be occasions to reduce your payment by finding a better interest rate than you have currently, which could free up additional cash flow and reduce the risk you must take on your dollars for you to maintain control. An example would be to use an equity line of credit that has a lower rate than the rate you pay on another loan. Perhaps you had to give up collateral to get the original loan, but if you were able to get a lower interest rate and improve your collateral position, you come out ahead. An equity line of credit usually cost nothing to put in place and can be a tremendous tool to ease your financial pressure when unexpected major capital purchases come along.

So let's say the money in your Investment Tank is doing well and earning a good return, so the thought of having to drain the tank to pay for a wedding makes little sense. Your cash flow is sufficient to cover your current lifestyle but you can't cash flow the entire cost of a wedding too. Pressure! Where will you get the money? Your daughter does not have time to wait for you to save $50,000 from your current cash flow once she shows you the engagement ring. Then you remember you have an equity line of credit at the bank and while they will not give you a signature loan for a wedding, they will loan you money using the equity in your house as collateral without you having to tell them why you need the money. Problem solved. Your daughter has a beautiful wedding and you enjoy the wedding rather than worrying about the cost. You know you can pay the loan off over time from monthly cash flow without having to reduce your contributions to your retirement accounts and your money is still compounding interest. Life is good. Your current financial obligation would be to pay just the interest due on the loan. At 3% that would mean you only need to come up with $1,500 to get you through the wedding ceremony giving you time to pay the balance as you go. If you want to pay off the wedding loan quicker, you can to restore your access to capital with the bank while you remain in control.

The one thing that can remove financial pressure in your life is access to capital. In our last example, you could be turned down at the bank for an equity line of credit if the mortgage market is not doing well. You are limited to borrowing only 50% of your qualified plan account dollars, assuming the plan allows for loans and any loan must be paid back in less than five years and if you quit your job or are terminated, the loan must be paid immediately which can cause a huge tax loss.

Having access to capital and alternatives to solve your MCPs provides for a content and stress free current lifestyle. Consider the accounts where you have money as playing cards. You have a financial issue that must be solved. You look at the cards you have in your hand and determine which card is the best to play that will cost you the least to solve the situation. If you have no cards in your hand or the cards you have do not allow you to get to the money you will experience financial pressure.

There is a great deal to know about your money and what you know may not be as important as what you don't know. Do you remember the child's game tic-tac-toe? Who won the first time you played? It was probably the person that showed you the game. They told you the object was to get three in a row, pretty simple. You played and lost regularly until you learned the strategies of the game. The same is true in the world of finance. The financial institutions have rules. Do they teach you the rules? No, you must learn as you play and unfortunately, you can lose thousands of dollars unnecessarily in the process.

This book was not designed to teach you all the rules but to give you solid financial information, so that you can play more efficiently. The rules change frequently and we recommend you find a financial services professional that can help you stay on top of things but you are ultimately the one responsible for how things turn out.

In the next chapter, we are going to introduce you to a process called the Private Reserve Strategy. To utilize this strategy, you will need to find an account to serve as your private reserve of capital that allows you easy access to your money through collateralization, unrestricted control and preferably earns compound interest uninterrupted.

Chapter 20: The Private Reserve Strategy

The Private Reserve Strategy is designed to help develop or improve one's financial position by helping them avoid or minimize unnecessary wealth transfers where possible, and accumulate an increasing pool of capital that provides easy accessibility through collateralization, unrestricted control and uninterrupted compounding.

Easy accessibility to your money plays an important role in reducing and eliminating the financial pressure that life can bring. Having money in accounts that you can't get to can cause not only financial stress but also cause unwanted expense and loss when forced to use other sources of capital to cover an unexpected major capital purchase. Although the money in your tanks is there mainly for your future, from time to time access to your money can relieve a great deal of pressure. Just knowing it is there if you need it and you can get to it anytime you wish is comforting. Draining a tank to access your money is less preferable than using other people's money especially when you can access their money at lower rates than you are earning on your money.

Collateralization allows you the ability to borrow against your capital and use OPM, or other people's money, allowing your future lifestyle dollars to continue compounding while paying over time for a current lifestyle expense from your current lifestyle dollars. Collateralization is a key part of the Private Reserve Strategy because it allows you access to capital without having to drain your tanks. Draining an account that is earning you interest has a cost. You save interest draining your tanks to pay cash for your purchase but you lose the interest those dollars would have earned had you left them in your tank. You never want to drain a tank to buy something that you need or want that you could finance with another lender at a lower rate than your money is earning. Have we made it clear that draining a tank to pay cash is financing – it is self-financing.

An example of collateralization you are familiar with would be when you purchase a home. You were required to make a down payment to serve as security for the loan. If you do not make your payments, the bank is entitled to take the property to satisfy your financial obligation. Banks will often require collateral to secure a business loan to secure their interest should you default. As we discussed earlier, credit cards, do not require collateralization and should not be used to finance major capital purchases or expenses that can't be paid off before interest charges are applied.

Unrestricted control allows access to your money on your terms. The financial institutions prefer to impose limitations on when and how much of your money you can access while your money is in their accounts. Higher return potential usually comes with less control and less accessibility. While return is important it is not the only factor you should consider in establishing an account to serve as your private reserve. When times are hard, control of your money is a tremendous stress reliever. I am sure you have heard the old saying "cash is king." It is an old saying and it is still true.

Uninterrupted compounding is a benefit to be desired. Compound interest has often been called the eighth wonder of the world. Accounts that can appreciate over time certainly have their place in your financial picture but they can also depreciate. Accounts that compound interest uninterrupted grow steadily over time and protect against loss. The longer you allow your money to grow, the better these types of accounts perform.

Whenever you borrow, you will be required to pay interest for the privilege of using someone else's money. When you use your money, putting what you took from your tanks has a tendency to not get back. If it does get put back it rarely gets put back at interest. It is easy to believe that because you are not having to pay interest you are not losing interest. You must not forget to pay back the interest you lost while the money was out of your account. It is important that you shop for the best loan option available to minimize unnecessary wealth transfers in interest payments. In the chapter on debt, we looked at someone who had no money in their Savings and Investment Tanks which offered few accessible options to secure a loan other than using credit cards. Borrowing with no collateral to be able to pay except for money you have yet to earn is the very definition of debt.

When you borrow and you have the capability to pay you are not in debt but you do have a liability. You have a mortgage loan on your house. The house is worth more than you owe. You have a liability but the asset value is worth more than the liability so you are not in debt. Living life near or on the "zero" line with no collateral capacity is stress ridden and just a step away from financial ruin.

The Private Reserve Strategy allows one access to capital through collateralization without having to disrupt the power of compounding interest on the money in their savings and investment accounts. Remember compound interest works best over time, uninterrupted. One of the major reasons for the lack of financial success is the killing of compounding on the money we are putting away for our future. When you drain the tank for a major capital purchase, you are killing compounding on the amount of money borrowed. Resetting compounding is like running in a race and half way through, going back to the beginning to get a drink and starting over. You are never going to win and you can't get back to the same position you were in before you left the race.

When you need access to capital and you have collateral you can shop for interest rates from other sources, preferably at lower interest rates than you are earning in your accounts. How much money you make is important when qualifying for a loan but even more important is how much money you have that is accessible. It sounds strange but lenders only want to loan money to those who do not need the money. Your character is another important factor in not only determining if you can get a loan but also the interest rate you will be charged. Lenders look at your credit history looking for indications that you are a person of character who pays all their bills and pays on time.

Lenders want two things. They want to earn interest and they want the amount of the loan secured in the event you were to default on the loan. Your goal should be similar to theirs. You want to earn a competitive rate of return on your money with little to no chance to lose. There is more opportunity in avoiding the losses than picking the winners.

The Private Reserve Strategy™

Private Reserve

PRS: 12/17 © MoneyTrax, Inc.

Let's look at a visual representation of how the Private Reserve Strategy works. In the above picture, you will notice the tank on the left represents your private reserve account, simply meaning an account you control that provides you with access to your money that is earning compound interest uninterrupted. You need to make a major capital purchase, so you go shopping to find a financial institution to loan you the money at a rate preferably lower than the interest you are earning on the dollars in your tanks. You borrow the money for your current lifestyle purchase from a lender and they take a lien against your private reserve account. You will have structured payments to the institution and as you pay off the loan and as the lien is reduced your collateral position is increased.

Up to this point, our focus has been on discussing how money works. We want to help you balance your current lifestyle desires and your future lifestyle requirement by improving efficiencies and minimizing unnecessary losses.

When someone comes along with information outside your box of knowledge, you have two choices. The first is to immediately dismiss the information and ignore it. The second is to get a bigger box. I will remind you that some of the information you are about to hear will be uncommon wisdom and require you to look at things from a different point of view.

Chapter 21: Choosing the Account for Your Private Reserve

Y ou should understand from our previous discussions about the Savings and Investment Tanks and that you need to have money in both. While dollars in the Investment Tank certainly offer a greater chance for higher returns, those accounts also have a greater opportunity for loss. There should be no question that dollars in the Investment Tank are for your future and need time to appreciate to produce gains. If you have an immediate need for capital, putting money in the Investment Tank and draining the tank to cover a pressing lifestyle expense is not a decision that will turn out in your favor. Unfortunately assets in the investment tank do not normally allow for you to borrow against them.

Just as there is no question that you should have money in your Investment Tank, there is no question that you should be setting aside money in your Savings Tank as well. The Diverter Valve in the model allows you to decide how much money you want to have in each tank. The Switch Valves allow you to move money between tanks to keep your allocation percentages at your desired levels. The best safe accounts to serve as your private reserve allow you easy access to your money through collateralization earning uninterrupted compound interest.

In this section, we are going to give you some direction on account options available for you to set up your private reserve account that can take care of your current lifestyle access to capital needs as well as provide a solid foundation for your long term future lifestyle.

When looking for an account to serve as your private reserve, you need to begin by looking for an account that has the benefits you want. Remember that there are basically three fundamental benefits that the account must be able to do to qualify as your private reserve before you even start looking at additional benefits that may be offered.

Those three things again are that the money in the tank must be easily accessible, can be collateralized, and must earn compound interest uninterrupted. While accounts that have the highest potential for return are primarily found in the yellow or Investment Tank your private reserve account should also provide reasonable return potential. Here is a list of benefits for you to use as a guide to determine if the account you are looking at is up to par. You will never find one account that gives you every benefit you want, so you should look for the account that gives you the most of what you want.

Private Reserve Account
Ideal Characteristics and Benefits

- Tax Deferred Growth
- Tax Free Distribution
- Competitive Return
- High Contributions
- Deductible Contributions
- Collateral Opportunities
- Safe Harbor
- No-Loss Provisions
- Guaranteed Loan Option
- Unstructured Loan Payments
- Liquidity, Use and Control
- Additional Benefits

PRS: 14/17 © MoneyTrax, Inc.

If you could have everything you want this list is a good place to start.

Deductible Contributions: Deductible contributions is a great benefit if you can find it but if you do you can be assured that the federal government is heavily involved with rules and regulations.

Tax Deferred: You definitely want the money in your account to grow tax deferred as opposed to taxable. Compounding interest is interrupted when a tax is paid. Remember, if you have to pay a tax you must calculate the cost of the tax plus the opportunity cost of what you could earn on those dollars had you not had to pay them. Deferring taxes is better than paying them because when you pay a tax those dollars are gone that could be working for you.

Tax Free Distribution: Tax deferred is better than taxable but both are inferior to tax free distribution.

Competitive Returns: Accounts that earn compound interest decrease the opportunity for loss.

High Contributions: The government does not have many rules about contributions to accounts where gains earned in the account create a tax. You will find many rules and regulations on accounts where interest grows tax deferred or the money comes out tax free and the allowable amount of contributions are usually limited.

Collateral Opportunities: This benefit is a must for the account you choose to be your private reserve. You must be able to borrow against the account to access capital to help you with the major capital purchases that will impact your current lifestyle from time to time allowing you access to your money without having to drain your tank.

Guaranteed Loan Options: This is another highly desirable benefit. You do not want to have to negotiate to get to your money it must be easily accessible at all times.

Unstructured Loan Payments: An account that will allow you to set the payback period and amount would provide a great deal of flexibility and control when you borrow.

Safe: A primary characteristic of the Safe Tank accounts is that those dollars must be safe from loss and you will need an account in the safe tank rather than the investment tank to serve as your private reserve. The cap on the top of the safe tank represents the fact that money in this tank cannot be lost.

No Loss Provisions: This means the money in the tank is safer than safe, meaning that there are contractual provisions in the account itself that guarantee no loss.

Liquidity, Use, and Control: The money in the account must be liquid, meaning you can easily get to it. You must be able to use the money for any purpose without qualifications or restrictions and you must be the one in control of the account, not the institution holding the money.

Additional benefits: The benefits mentioned above are the most important but there are accounts that offer specialized benefits. Suit protection would be one such benefit, so the money in your account is free from creditors. Also, disability protection on contributions to your account if you can't continue to make your contributions is a powerful benefit.

So now you have a better idea of your perfect list of benefits and you would want them all if you could wave your magic wand and have anything you want. With your benefits list in mind, let's take a look at some of the accounts that could operate as your private reserve and allow you to see how many benefits are offered in each account.

Potential Private Reserve candidates:

401(k) and Qualified Plans

The first one we will look at is your 401(k) or Qualified Plans accounts including IRAs. These type of accounts start off with a winner in that they offer tax deductable contributions. Remember what we learned in the chapter on qualified plans. You may "deduct" the amount of your contribution from your earned income but that does not mean you do not have any tax liability. It simply means that you can pay your taxes due later. The big question is what will your tax rate be when you take the money out of these types of accounts?

IRAs offer competitive return potential because these accounts allow for many different investment options. We believe that all money in these accounts should be viewed in the Investment Tank because of the uncertainty of the future tax liability, even though you can put money in safe accounts inside the plan. Choosing to put money in accounts with low return potential inside qualified plans and give up access to your capital until age 59 ½ may not be your best alternative since the purpose of these plans is more for long term growth. Another thought to consider is why would you want money in safe accounts inside a qualified plan that offers limited returns and no access with the potential to pay higher taxes at the time of withdrawal? It would seem that you would be better served to keep your safe money in an account that is easily accessible with little or no future tax liability. Qualified plans may offer loan provisions if listed in the plan documents but as you can see in the chart there are many things to consider before taking a loan from these types of accounts.

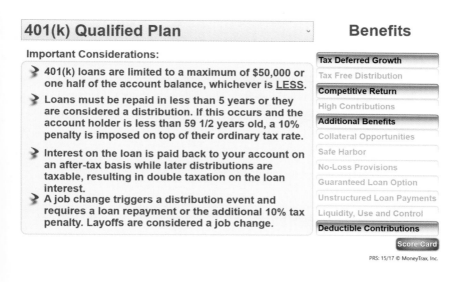

401(k) Qualified Plan

Important Considerations:

- ❯ 401(k) loans are limited to a maximum of $50,000 or one half of the account balance, whichever is LESS.
- ❯ Loans must be repaid in less than 5 years or they are considered a distribution. If this occurs and the account holder is less than 59 1/2 years old, a 10% penalty is imposed on top of their ordinary tax rate.
- ❯ Interest on the loan is paid back to your account on an after-tax basis while later distributions are taxable, resulting in double taxation on the loan interest.
- ❯ A job change triggers a distribution event and requires a loan repayment or the additional 10% tax penalty. Layoffs are considered a job change.

Benefits

Tax Deferred Growth

Tax Free Distribution

Competitive Return

High Contributions

Additional Benefits

Collateral Opportunities

Safe Harbor

No-Loss Provisions

Guaranteed Loan Option

Unstructured Loan Payments

Liquidity, Use and Control

Deductible Contributions

Score Card

PRS: 15/17 © MoneyTrax, Inc.

These types of accounts do meet one of the three fundamental qualifications to be considered as a good private reserve account which is the money in these accounts is accessible, although there are restrictions. You can only borrow 50% of the accounts value, with a maximum loan amount of $50,000. If you do borrow from your 401(k), you must pay the loan off with interest in less than five years. Should you quit or be fired from your job, the entire balance of the loan is due within sixty days and layoffs are considered a job change. You must pay back the loan with after tax dollars and those same dollars will then be taxable to you after age 59 ½ when you can take withdrawals. However, they do not offer the ability to collateralize the value of the account with other financial institutions, regardless of the amount you have in them. The underlying investment accounts typically appreciate or depreciate because of market fluctuations and do not compound interest uninterrupted.

Compare the benefits highlighted with those that are not on the qualified plan list. Using a qualified plan account as your private reserve provides four of the twelve benefits on the list.

Certificates of Deposit

CDs, as they are commonly called, provide two of the three fundamental functions to be a private reserve account. The money in these accounts is accessible, although not without a penalty for early withdrawal. They do compound interest, if you allow the interest earned to roll back into the account but not interrupted because you must pay taxes on the interest earned annually. It is rare that one would reduce the value of their CD to pay the tax liability due on the interest earned during the year. The most common is to pay the tax due from current lifestyle which reduces lifestyle cash flow. You can collateralize a loan against the money you have in a CD but you must negotiate the loan and your loan request can be denied.

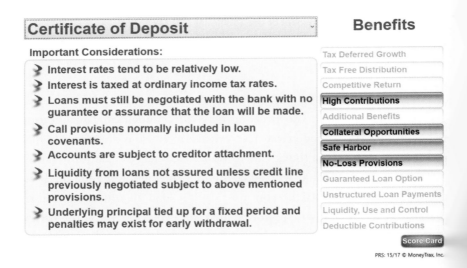

Certificate of Deposit | **Benefits**

Important Considerations:

- Interest rates tend to be relatively low.
- Interest is taxed at ordinary income tax rates.
- Loans must still be negotiated with the bank with no guarantee or assurance that the loan will be made.
- Call provisions normally included in loan covenants.
- Accounts are subject to creditor attachment.
- Liquidity from loans not assured unless credit line previously negotiated subject to above mentioned provisions.
- Underlying principal tied up for a fixed period and penalties may exist for early withdrawal.

Benefits list:
Tax Deferred Growth
Tax Free Distribution
Competitive Return
High Contributions
Additional Benefits
Collateral Opportunities
Safe Harbor
No-Loss Provisions
Guaranteed Loan Option
Unstructured Loan Payments
Liquidity, Use and Control
Deductible Contributions

Score Card

PRS: 15/17 © MoneyTrax, Inc.

Before you run off to the bank, there are a few things you should consider. The interest rates tend to be relatively low in today's market and rise and fall very slowly over time. Any interest earned is taxed as ordinary income and you need to consider the opportunity cost of taxes paid that could have been avoided. You can put as much in a CD as you wish, although they are not protected from loss by the FDIC in amounts exceeding $250,000. For this reason, additional CD accounts are recommended when contributions and values exceed the $250,000 amount. These accounts are safe from loss at lower amounts than $250,000; however, in low interest markets, some would argue they are not safe from loss if they do not at least keep up with the rate of inflation.

To borrow against the value of a CD, you must negotiate the loan with the bank with no guarantee that you will get the loan just because you have a CD. The bank usually has the ability to call the loan and there are time constraints set at the beginning of the loan and penalties if broken. These accounts are subject to creditors and can be attachable in the event of a suit.

CDs provide four of the twelve benefits on the list of benefits.

Money Market/Savings Accounts

Money market and savings accounts also meet two of the three fundamental requirements. They are on the top of the list for accessibility but the rate of return is normally low and they do not compound interest uninterrupted because any interest gained though small is taxed annually. Money in these accounts can be collateralized but they are primarily used to put money away for a short period of time that allows instant access to capital. Investors like to utilize these accounts when saving to participate in an investment opportunity that requires a

> **Money in these accounts can be collateralized but they are primarily used to put money away for a short period of time that allows instant access to capital.**

sizable monetary investment. These accounts are also used to hold money in an emergency fund where one would have three to six months of income set aside to cover unexpected situations that require immediate access to capital.

These accounts may also be a temporary short term holding tank to accumulate money for a current lifestyle expense in the immediate future or until there is enough in the tank to move to the Investment Tank in search of greater return potential. It is not normally an account designed for long term accumulation.

Money market accounts provide five of the twelve benefits on the list.

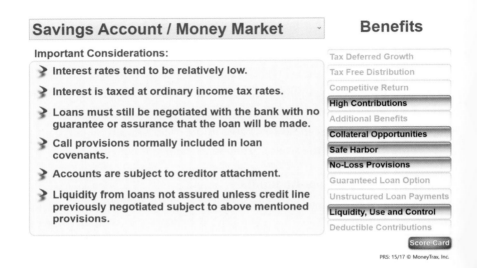

Margin Account on a Stock Portfolio

You will find a margin account in the Investment Tank rather than the Savings Tank. The term margin suggests an immediate need for capital which when executed provides a collateralized loan against the value of the stock portfolio. These accounts do offer immediate access to capital but usually limited to 50% of the underlying stock value. You can borrow against the account value using the stock as collateral, which does allow the stock to continue to potentially earn a greater value than the loan interest charged, but stock does not compound interest uninterrupted. The value of the stock portfolio appreciates or depreciates, depending on the market.

While these accounts do offer two of the three fundamental prerequisites of a private reserve account, they do bring risk into the equation and loans from these accounts would not be recommended for current lifestyle expenses. The main reason is because decline in the underlying stock value could result in margin call requiring the sale of the underlying stock which could be undesirable financially and have a negative impact on one's financial future.

Borrowing money against your stock to purchase more stock is the normal use of these types of loans and while the opportunity for greater gain may be high, so is the risk. We would never recommend taking a margin loan to purchase a current lifestyle expense and those who consider borrowing to buy investment products do so understanding that if their stock value goes down, they still are responsible for the loan. A call on a margin loan requires the loan be paid immediately and in cash.

The private reserve strategy is designed to help you through life with the major capital purchases and current lifestyle expenses you will need to make. While technically a margin account could be used as a private reserve account, we would not recommend them to be used in this way.

Margin Account on Stock Portfolio

Benefits

Important Considerations:

- Amount available typically half the value of the stock portfolio.
- Amount available can change subject to Federal Regulations.
- Decline in underlying stock portfolio could result in a margin call.
- Margin calls require cash deposits or stock portfolio sales (usually in a depressed market).
- Margin call sales could trigger capital gains tax on stock sales.
- Loan rates usually tied to LIBOR and can fluctuate.
- Hedge fund shorting could trigger decline in the underlying security value and cause a margin call.

Tax Deferred Growth
Tax Free Distribution
Competitive Return
High Contributions
Additional Benefits
Collateral Opportunities
Safe Harbor
No-Loss Provisions
Guaranteed Loan Option
Unstructured Loan Payments
Liquidity, Use and Control
Deductible Contributions

Score Card

PRS: 15/17 © MoneyTrax, Inc.

Real Estate

While investment real estate may be your investment of choice and for many can be a good investment, borrowing against it can at times be difficult or impossible. Real estate purchases would be in the Investment Tank because it is an asset with value that brings risk into the discussion. To borrow against investment real estate will require appraisals and usually large amounts of time negotiating with the lender not to mention providing all of your financial information for review.

Home equity loans on your primary residence can offer immediate access to capital once in place and these loans are collateralized against the value of your house. To receive capital for this type of loan, you must have sufficient equity and solid credit. The bank making the loan can terminate the loan or choose not to renew. These loans usually have caps but should be sufficient to cover most current lifestyle expenses.

Once the loan has been negotiated and approved by the bank, access to money is as simple as writing a check. There are no restrictions on what you can purchase with the money once you receive the loan; however, the bank may ask you why you want the loan at the time you request it. If you can qualify for one without paying to have it, it would be a good idea to have in place, even though you have no need for the money today. Access to capital may be a benefit you never have to use but if you are in need of capital this can be a good source. Repayment of these loans usually only requires at a minimum the interest to be paid allowing you to repay the principal on your terms.

> **There are no restrictions on what you can purchase with the money once you receive the loan; however, the bank may ask you why you want the loan at the time you request it.**

Home equity loans can provide access to capital and the house is used as collateral but the house does not compound interest uninterrupted. The house appreciates or depreciates. One would hope that while they are paying off their home equity loan, the value of the house has increased but that is not guaranteed. The housing market could drop causing the value of the house to depreciate, meaning that further access to capital using the house as collateral could be unavailable.

Real Estate Equity w/HELOC

Benefits

Important Considerations:

➤ HELOCs must be granted by banks and are conditional on credit worthiness and bank liquidity.

➤ HELOCs in place may be revoked at any time at the discretion of the bank if no loans are outstanding.

➤ Most HELOCs have call provisions.

➤ Given the fluctuation of house valuations, the amount of equity available for some borrowers could be insufficient for their needs.

➤ HELOCs generally have caps on the amount of available credit.

Tax Deferred Growth
Tax Free Distribution
Competitive Return
High Contributions
Additional Benefits
Collateral Opportunities
Safe Harbor
No-Loss Provisions
Guaranteed Loan Option
Unstructured Loan Payments
Liquidity, Use and Control
Deductible Contributions

Score Card

PRS: 15/17 © MoneyTrax, Inc.

Home equity loans provide two of the twelve benefits listed.

The last account we want to discuss will be covered in the following chapter because it offers the greatest number of benefits of all the potential accounts discussed. It also deserves closer attention because it is perhaps the one financial product where everyone has an opinion but few really have a full understanding of how to utilize it to its maximum potential.

Keep in mind that all money must reside somewhere. Once you get it, you must put it somewhere, even if it is under your mattress. Deciding where to put it is the dilemma but putting it under your mattress should not be one of your options. It may see complicated when you are bombarded by the thousands of savings and investment opportunities that exist but breaking your decision down into how the money must go into the account and how it comes out should make your decision a bit easier. Learning these following fundamentals can help you determine what type of account offers the greatest number of benefits you are looking for from the places you put your money.

There are some accounts that are funded with aftertax dollars and your partner the federal government also wants a piece of the gains you earn on those dollars.

Money can go directly from your hands into accounts that are designed to grow over time but do not allow access to the money until your retirement without penalty.

At the other end of the spectrum are accounts that allow access but little to no opportunity for growth.

There are accounts that can be funded with before tax dollars that are required to be taxed at the time of withdrawal.

There are others that are funded with aftertax dollars that allow tax free withdrawals.

You will most likely have money in many or all of the fundamental account types just mentioned. The purpose of having some of your money in a private reserve account is to allow you easy access to some of your money that also provides other benefits in addition to a competitive return without the risk of loss.

Chapter 21: The Most Powerful Tank in the World

To help explain this statement let's go back again to our golf analogy. When you think about golf there is one club designed to hit the ball a long way. That club is called the "driver." If we think about the relationship of golf and your finances the driver would represent rate of return. Every golfer wants to hit their drive just a little longer and every investor would like to earn higher returns. You need products in the Investment Tank that will help you get off the tee and down the fairway with positive return potential.

Have you ever lost a ball with a driver? If you have ever hit a golf ball with a driver, you would know the answer is yes. That is why golf balls come in packs of twelve. The driver has the greatest potential of all the clubs to hit the ball the farthest but it is also the hardest club to control. If you hit the ball straight it can leave you with an easy approach shot to the green but when you don't it can put you in big trouble. An errant shot in the woods, a sand trap, or in the water results in extra strokes and if you should lose the ball a two stroke penalty. Avoiding losses is the name of the game in golf as well as managing your money. More tournaments are won from avoiding mistakes than hitting fantastic shots.

Few if any of us could ever say we lost a ball with a putter. If you asked every tour professional on the LPGA or PGA tour which of the 14 clubs they are allowed to have in their bag is the most valuable they will all say without reservation, the putter. The putter would never be mentioned in a distance conversation. The putter, although it does not hit the ball far, can save you strokes on the green that can make up for mistakes you might have made with your driver. In golf you need both of these clubs in your bag and the same is true financially. You need both of these clubs if you are to be successful.

There are limitless financial opportunities to serve as your investment driver but there are very few products that qualify with the same safety features of the putter. We looked at the accounts in the last chapter that could perform as your private reserve account and permanent life insurance is the option that provides the greatest number of benefits. Permanent life insurance is a solid choice for your putter.

The most powerful tank in the world is the Safe Tank filled with permanent life insurance. Perhaps when you read the words life insurance you wanted to close the book but don't. Be honest with yourself, is life insurance something that you know in your circle of knowledge or something that you vaguely know about, or is it in your blind spot? The reason permanent life insurance makes the Safe Tank powerful is that it is the only product that can guarantee that what you want to happen financially will happen, even in the event you are not here to see it happen.

When you compare the internal rate of return of a life insurance contract against the potential returns of other investment opportunities I would agree that life insurance would not even make the list. That would be like comparing which club could hit the ball the farthest, the driver or the putter. However access to cash values allows you to participate in any investment opportunity you desire in search of potentially higher returns than the insurance carrier is paying inside the contract.

In addition permanent life insurance policies allow for easy access to capital to take care of any major capital purchases. They also allow you to collateralize a loan against cash values and pay back the loan to the insurance company over time on your schedule and they compound interest uninterrupted.

You will need money in the Safe Tank providing access to capital allowing you to handle the major capital purchases that come along from time to time that can disrupt your current lifestyle and cash flow. While your focus on dollars in the Investment Tank is primarily about return, the focus on dollars in the Safe Tank is more about the benefits—access to the cash value allows you to have both. Accounts in the Investment Tank have the potential for greater returns but offer few benefits. Accounts in the Safe Tank offer less return potential but a greater amount of benefits.

When you understand how to utilize the power of the life insurance contract you will want all you can get. You would have to admit that any golf club in the hands of a professional would perform better than in the hands of someone who plays every other weekend. The power is not so much in the club or the product if you will, but in the swing.

A permanent life insurance policy, properly funded, can provide competitive tax favored cash accumulation and access to capital to invest in any opportunity or cover any major capital purchase along life's journey. In addition it can fill both tanks instantly should you die which will take you a lifetime of earnings to accomplish should you live. No other product has such a benefit.

It may surprise you to learn that the largest institutions in America, including banks, own billions in life insurance as their private reserve. What do they know that perhaps you don't know? In this chapter, you will gain a deeper understanding of permanent life insurance and how this product can solve your access to capital issues and provide eleven of the twelve benefits on the benefits list. Knowing how to use this product to accomplish your financial and personal goals in life is much more valuable than simply having life insurance for the death protection.

If what you thought to be true turned out not to be true, when would you want to know? Keep reading.

Permanent life insurance offers all three of the primary fundamentals necessary for an account to perform as a private reserve account for your money. The number one fundamental and a must is the immediate and easy accessibility to capital. The second requirement is that the money in the account must be accessible through collateralization allowing both borrowed and non-borrowed funds to continue earning interest and the third requirement is the account must compound interest uninterrupted.

I have always been puzzled that it seems that life insurance companies have been so unsuccessful in telling the American public how their product works in such a way that is easily understood. In the following discussion, I will share the fundamental things you should know when considering using permanent life insurance as your private reserve account. When you are finished reading you may know more about life insurance than many agents and at the very least you will know more than they have been telling you.

To begin, it is important that you understand than no life insurance contract can be considered an investment. I know that many of the product names given by these insurance companies could lead you to think otherwise, but they are not investments and not in the Investment Tank. Permanent life insurance is in the Safe Tank. That being said, you should also understand that with the access to capital in a permanent life insurance policy, you are not limited to the internal returns provided through the insurance carrier but you are open to every investment opportunity you desire. Many business men and women have utilized their cash value to build very successful companies that produce much greater returns than the insurance company could offer through the insurance product alone. One name you will easily recognize was Walt Disney. What do you think the rate of return on that investment has been?

Before I share with you how a permanent life insurance policy can work for you I want to share a real life example of how the internal rate of return of the policy has little to do with the rate of return you can earn if you know how to use this product. Unfortunately rate of return is as far as many people look.

I was living in Louisiana when I met with a gentleman who was interested in doing some financial planning. He said he was not interested in the stock market because he was earning more return with his money in the freezer. Being an advisor, I could not wait to hear this story. He said he keeps about $100,000 in his freezer. I am thinking this guy is crazy. He could be earning at least some interest if he had it in the bank.

He went on to tell me he likes to fix up muscle cars. He goes to car shows looking for cars where he can restore the car and make a profit. He said he takes his $100,000 in a Maxwell House coffee can out of the freezer and buys a car for about $30,000, brings it home, puts about $20,000 more into restoring it to like new and sells it for $75,000. He said he does at least two cars a year. He asked me if I knew of a mutual fund account I could recommend where he could do better than that. I could not.

I learned a great deal from him that day. The Maxwell House coffee can where he kept his money had nothing to do with the rate of return he was earning. A Folger's coffee can would work just as well. What mattered was what he did with the money. When I shared with him that a permanent life insurance contract would allow him to do the same thing allowing easy access to his money, earn interest, be safer and provide more benefits, he wanted to know more.

Let's begin our discussion and let me share with you what I told him that day about permanent life insurance.

There is the minimum one can pay for a given amount of insurance coverage at a specific age, and the maximum one can pay. Who determines the minimum? The insurance company. At the other end of the spectrum is the maximum one can pay for a given amount of coverage, and who determines that besides you? The government. The fact that the federal government limits how much money one can put in a life insurance policy says what about it? It must be….goooood. And it must be good in relationship to one subject: taxes.

Basically, the government regulates the upper limit of tax advantaged growth they will allow and the policy holder still have access to the cash value. Policies outside this allowable corridor are determined to be a Modified Endowment Contract or MEC, which simply means the government will treat the insurance contract like they do qualified plans with the same rules, regulations, and penalties and gains about the amount of contributions will be taxed if you terminate the contract. Death benefits come to the beneficiary tax free even if the policy has been deemed a modified endowment contract.

There is almost an infinite amount of premium options that can be charged between the minimum and maximum for any given amount of coverage. As mentioned earlier, the insurance companies determine the minimum. They have actuaries that calculate the least amount of premium they can charge and still make a profit. They understand the opportunity cost which means they have factored in the time value of the premium and designed the product to provide value to their customers and make money on the product when sold.

In the 1980s, the government drew the line that determined the maximum amount of contributions allowable for a given face amount of coverage at a specific age. They accomplished this with two laws: the Technical and Miscellaneous Revenue Act of 1988, or TAMRA, and the Deficit Reduction Act of 1984, or DEFRA. These two laws basically said "wait just a minute— we need to limit the amount of allowable contributions to a life insurance policy because if we don't it will hinder contributions to qualified plans." Who would put money in qualified plans if you could get the same results with life insurance and still have access to the money? The thing that keeps a life insurance policy from being an investment is that it must provide death protection in addition to being an accumulation account and not just an account to accumulate money on a tax favored basis.

What does the government encourage you to do, besides pay taxes? Put money in a qualified plan account and defer the taxes. Samples of these accounts include 401(k)s, IRAs, SEPs and 403(b) plans, to name just a few.

What do qualified plans do? If you remember from our earlier discussion, the number one response is that they defer taxes. They do defer taxes but they also defer the tax calculation. Perhaps a clearer word the government could have used would have been post-pone. Qualified plans are not tax savings plans but rather, tax deferred savings plans. The government did not say "you do not owe the tax." They said, "you can pay the tax later." At what bracket? That is a good question and the questions you should be asking when considering these type accumulation accounts. This is not to say qualified plans are bad. However, it is important that you know and understand exactly what they do.

Now, let's get back to life insurance.

Let's assume you could pay $500 for $500,000 of insurance coverage, at your age or you could pay $10,000 for the same amount of coverage. Which would you choose? Being bargain shoppers, most of us would probably say $500. Less is best when it comes to cost, right?

Let's say the $500 represents the lowest premium one can pay for $500,000 of coverage at a given age. The lowest premium in the life insurance world is known as term insurance. It provides one benefit: death protection. Term insurance offers death protection for the least expensive initial cost.

Financially, the best day to own term insurance is which day? If you guessed the day you die, you were not even close. The best day financially to own a term life insurance policy is the first day. That's right; it is the first day you get it.

Had you purchased the policy today, received approval, signed the delivery receipt, paid the first premium and died on the way home from your agent's office—you can't get better than that. Since the face amount or death benefit of a term policy does not increase over time with additional payments, every payment made actually reduces the amount of coverage you have in force because some of the benefit is your money. If the best day to own a term policy is the first day, it means that every day you own it, the policy becomes worth less, costing you more.

In addition to determining the cost of term insurance, one must also factor in the opportunity cost of owning this product. Remember that the cost is not just the amount you paid in premiums, but what those dollars could have earned had you not bought the coverage and taken the risk yourself which we are not suggesting you do. In other words, if you are earning 6% in another account, then the true cost of your term coverage should include the premiums factored over time at the same 6% interest rate. The opportunity cost does not stop when you stop making payments. Those dollars spent are gone and will never return.

Here is something you may not know about term life insurance. Penn State University completed a study on term insurance policies where they discovered that:

- more than 90% of all term policies are terminated or converted to permanent coverage —45% within the first year, and 72% within the first 3 years,
- less than 1 term policy in 10 survives the period for which it is written,
- after 15 to 20 years of exposure, less than 1% of all term policies are still in force, and
- only 1% of all term insurance in force resulted in death claims.

What does this mean? It means with term insurance, you will most likely pay more than you receive.

But permanent coverage is more expensive. For an insurance company to talk you into putting $10,000 in a permanent life policy with the same amount of coverage that you could get for $500, they would have to come up with some serious benefits… agreed?

So let's forget about insurance again for just a minute and talk about benefits. In the private reserve discussion we were looking for an account where your money is accessible, that you can borrow against, and compounds interest uninterrupted. In addition, you would like to have as many benefits as possible in addition to achieving an acceptable rate of return.

As you look for a suitable account to put your money what benefits would you want? Remember all money must reside somewhere so it makes perfect sense to maximize those dollars by getting the most benefits for your dollar.

Put a check mark by the benefits of those you would like to have as you read through the list of benefits.

❏ the money in the account grows tax deferred as opposed to taxable
❏ tax-free distributions
❏ a competitive rate of return
❏ an account that does not limit the size of your contributions
❏ an account that would continue making your contributions if you can't
❏ an account free from creditors
❏ collateral opportunities allowing you to borrow against the account
❏ a safe account
❏ no loss provisions (meaning you can't lose your money)
❏ guaranteed loan options
❏ unstructured loan payments—you determine the payment schedule and amount
❏ deductible contributions

Obviously you would want the maximum amount of benefits possible. As we have seen from the benefits discussion in our last chapter there are no accounts that provide every benefit on the list. Permanent Life insurance provides eleven of the twelve on the list and the following chart compares the benefits available for all the accounts that we discussed in the previous chapter that could possibly work as your private reserve.

	PLI	HELOC	Margin	CD	Money Market	401(k)
Tax Deferred Growth	Y	Y	N	N	N	Y
Tax Free Distribution	Y	N	N	N	N	N
Competitive Return	Y	N	Y	N	N	Y
High Contributions	Y	N	Y	Y	Y	N
Additional Benefits	Y	N	N	N	N	Y
Collateral Opportunities	Y	Y	Y	Y	Y	N
Safe Harbor	Y	N	N	Y	Y	N
No-Loss Provisions	Y	N	N	Y	Y	N
Guaranteed Loan Option	Y	N	Y	N	N	N
Unstructured Loan Payments	Y	N	N	N	N	N
Liquidity, Use and Control	Y	N	Y	N	Y	N
Deductible Contributions	N	N	N	N	N	Y

PRSC: 1/1 © MoneyTrax, Inc.

Permanent life insurance contracts offer all the benefits listed earlier, except that the contributions to a life insurance contract outside of a qualified plan are not deductible. Deductions are a great benefit but simply post-pone taxes until later. When deciding on where to put your money you should consider the list of benefits and determine the benefits you want in your private reserve account.

There is only one product that offers the majority of the benefits on the list—and it is permanent life insurance. However, not just any type of insurance contract will do. Life insurance policies that are minimally funded only provide minimum levels of benefits. So financially, the best policy is the one that has the highest premium for the least amount of death protection. At this level, just below the government limit, the policy preforms at its maximum potential providing access to the capital and tax deferred growth without government interference.

Remember the government "drew the line" that determined the maximum amount of contributions allowable for a given face amount of coverage. Contributions over this line create a Modified Endowment Contract or MEC. However, contributions made right up to this line without going over create a different type of MEC that we call the Maximum Efficient Contract.

Before you decide that the fact that life insurance premiums are not deductible is a deal killer there is something you need to know. It may surprise you to learn that there is little difference between deductible and non-deductible contributions assuming the same tax rate at the time of contribution and withdrawal. In fact, tax deductible contributions that grow tax deferred and come out taxable are exactly the same as aftertax contributions that grow tax deferred and come out tax free, assuming the same tax brackets and investment interest rate.

How do traditional qualified plans compare to roth qualified plans?

Annual Contribution	$10,000
Current Tax Bracket	30.00%
Withdrawal Tax Bracket	30.00%
Years Until Withdrawal	30
Investment Return	5.00%

	Tax Def. Cont Taxable WD	After Tax Cont Tax Free WD
Equivalent Contribution	$10,000	$7,000
Gross Withdrawal	$697,608	$488,326
Amount Due IRS	$209,282	$0
Actual Net Withdrawal	$488,326	$488,326

QP: 6/8 © MoneyTrax, Inc.

You should also know that as you move from the highest possible premium to the lowest, the value of the benefits decrease. The higher the premium, the higher the level of each benefit received, until you reach the MEC line. Up to that line, but not over, is the position that provides the greatest amount of benefits a life insurance contract has to offer while still providing the three key benefits necessary to be an effective private reserve account, a maximum efficient contract. These policies allow for the greatest potential return providing the least amount of coverage.

There are circumstances where one needs permanent death protection and a low-level premium is desirable. When coverage is needed for a short period of time, term coverage may be the best immediate temporary solution even though the dollars spent have little chance to return. There are products that will provide the highest amount of death protection with a level premium which will providing minimum benefits if death protection not accumulation is the primary concern.

If death protection and accumulation are what you are looking for you will want a policy that allows for the highest premium contribution with the least amount of coverage to make the policy preform at its maximum potential. To keep policies from becoming government MEC contracts, the face amount increases each year along with the increase in cash values.

If you are looking for a place to accumulate money that provides the highest level of benefits mentioned at their maximum level, permanent life insurance can be a solid choice. Currently, we know of no other financial product that offers these same benefits at the same levels.

Insurance companies limit the amount of death protection one can purchase—known as the "face amount" based on:

* present age
* mortality costs
* current assets
* income

You should understand that it is impossible to leave someone rich through the proceeds of a life insurance contract. Like car insurance, you can't profit from a loss. You can only purchase enough coverage to return to the place you were before the claim. Don't forget we are all on the way to uninsurable and there will come a time when you will not be able to get it regardless of how much money you have.

How much insurance should you have? We discussed the answer to this question in the section on protection with term insurance and I am sure you have not forgotten about the plane that landed on the Hudson River in New York. Suppose you were one of those passengers on the plane that day. When you heard the news from pilot Sully that the plane was going down, how much life insurance would you have bought at that very moment? Would you have been more concerned about the price or the amount of coverage?

It is interesting that our minds seem to think more clearly in times of crisis than in times of comfort. Our recommendation about the amount of coverage you should have is that you should own all the insurance companies will allow you to own or as much as you want.

There is one last thing you need to understand about life insurance and that has to do with policy loans. Unrestricted access to the cash value is a powerful benefit but often misunderstood and miscommunicated by insurance agents. The company will loan you money using your cash value as collateral. You do not borrow "from" your policy but "against" it. The power of the benefit is that your cash value is earning interest on borrowed and non-borrowed funds and as you pay off the loan to the insurance company your collateral capacity is increased.

The key point I want you to see is that your future is still moving forward when you take a loan against the policy for a major capital purchase. You did not have to drain the tank you were able to borrow against it allowing your current lifestyle cash flow to cover the expense. Having easy access relieves a great deal of stress when those major capital purchases come along knowing you can get to money. Before you borrow against your policy from the insurance company you should look for opportunities to borrow from other lenders at a lower rate than the insurance company is going to charge. Remember loans with the insurance company come with unstructured payments while loans with other lenders most often require structured payments.

The Switch Valves that allow money to flow between your tanks. You have the ability to borrow against your cash value and move money to the investment tank for higher return potential but don't forget that requires risk. Money can also flow from the investment tank to the safe tank when you have enough money at risk and are looking to move to a safer financial position.

All money must reside somewhere and make sure that if you choose to use a permanent life insurance contract as your private reserve, that what you want to happen will happen.

Summary: Golden Nuggets

We have covered a great deal of information in this book and it may be a book that you will need to read a few times. The summary is a listing from the beginning to the end of the financial truths, concepts, and strategies discussed we call golden nuggets. Just as a prospector is looking for little golden nuggets you should be looking to become more efficient in your Personal Economic Model by identifying the areas where you could be losing money unknowingly and unnecessarily. Few prospectors in the California gold rush made a fortune by finding huge nuggets of gold sitting in plain sight sitting on top of the ground. They had to dig and look closely to find bits and pieces here and there. It was hard work.

As you look to find areas to be more efficient you will have to work as well. We trust that this book has provided you information that will help you better identify where the money may be hiding in areas where you are potentially losing unknowingly and unnecessarily and improve your prospecting efforts in finding money.

This list of nuggets should allow you to quickly find the conversation you would like to read again.

We trust that the Personal Economic Model has provided clarity to help you better understand cash flow and inspire you to continue or begin balancing your Current Lifestyle desires with you Future Lifestyle requirements.

Golden Nuggets:

"There is more to be gained by avoiding the losses than picking the winners."
Introduction

The road to your financial destination grows steeper and steeper the longer you postpone getting started. *Page 10*

The money that will pass through your hands is finite. *Page 14*

Begin your financial planning with the end in mind. *Page 14*

Your job is to balance your current lifestyle desires with your future lifestyle requirements. *Page 17*

The key thing to walk away with about Current Lifestyle is that this is the natural flow for your money and any money that flows through this tube once spent is gone forever. *Page 19*

You can't spend everything you make and live that way forever. *Page 20*

Access to capital also serves as the number one factor in reducing financial stress on the model when major capital purchases pop up from time to time. *Page 24*

Avoiding losses is our preferred recommendation to maximizing your wealth potential. *Page 25*

A major capital purchase is anything that you can't afford to pay for in full with Monthly Cash Flow. *Page 26*

Compound interest over time, uninterrupted, now that is something to be desired. *Page 25*

Balance is the key to your financial success, like it is in most things in life. *Page 29*

You can find an advisor to help you manage your money but you are going to have to manage your lifestyle. *Page 29*

If something can take what you have from you, it is not really yours. *Page 31*

There is more opportunity in avoiding the losses than there is in picking the winners. *Page 32*

No matter how much you make, it is not unlimited. *Page 35*

Major Capital Purchases are anything that you can't afford to pay for in full with monthly cash flow. *Page 40*

If you are not tracking your monthly spending, you should. *Page 40*

When you are under financial pressure, it is difficult to think as clearly as when you are not. *Page 40*

Uncontrolled spending is an unsustainable practice for both the government and you as well. *Page 44*

Your financial future depends solely on what you pump into the Savings and Investment Tanks. *Page 49*

The truth is you cannot afford to lose, EVER. *Page 51*

Opportunity Cost. If you lose a dollar, you not only lost the dollar, but you lost what it could have earned for you had you not lost it. *Page 51*

Your success depends less on the "club," and more on the "swing." *Page 53*

The answer is not in the products but the process. *Page 53*

It is interesting that many people spend more time planning their annual vacation or cutting their grass than they spend planning their financial future. *Page 56*

Keep in mind the dollars you spend on lifestyle will never return. *Page 57*

The only thing that will help your future is filling your Savings and Investment Tanks. *Page 57*

There is a difference between average and actual returns *Page 60*

Just how much money are you willing to lose? *Page 66*

Do you save first then spend or ...*Page 66*

You finance everything you buy. *Page 111*

You either pay interest or you give up the ability to earn interest. *Page 111*

You self-financed the purchase *Page 111*

Control of your money may be even more valuable than the return on your money. *Page 112*

The real issue is not what you buy, but how to pay for it. *Page 114*

This is why we said that if you don't like paying interest, you must like losing interest. *Page 115*

The Debtor works to spend. *Page 120*

The Saver saves to avoid paying interest. *Page 120*

The Wealth Creator saves; they earn a reasonable rate of return on their money, and they collateralize lifestyle purchases using other people's money leaving their money in their tanks to serve as security for a loan. *Page 120*

When the Debtor borrows, they borrow from a lender, usually at the highest market rates *Page 121*

When the Saver borrows, they borrow from their own account and pay cash. They self-finance. *Page 121*

The Wealth Creator borrows from a lender at negotiated rates using their money as collateral to continue earning compound interest on their Future Lifestyle savings and investment dollars. *Page 121*

The mortgage payments you make in the early years of your mortgage are the most valuable dollars you will ever earn. *Page 130*

Your home actually costs you more the faster you pay it off because you are using your money valuable dollars. *Page 131*

Money in your house does not compound interest; it appreciates or depreciates. *Page 133*

The value of your house will be the same if you have your house paid in full or financed 100%. *Page 133*

If you finance with a lending institution, you transfer interest for the privilege of using their money. If you pay cash, or self-finance, you save interest, but you lose interest as well, because that money is not earning anything for you. *Page 135*

It is impossible to pay off your sleep habit. *Page 136*

Your home appreciates the same whether you have it paid off or financed 100%. *Page 137*

There is greater risk to earn any given rate of return over a shorter period than a longer period. *Page 139*

Having your home paid for is a safe financial position, but paid for without control may not be as safe as you once thought or it could be. *Page 140*

How does the thought of having to qualify to access your money sound? *Page 141*

When you need access to money, the lender is in the driver's seat. *Page 143*

Accounts that promise higher returns or tax advantages often come with reduced access to your money. *Page 156*

Given a choice, deferring taxes is better than paying them annually and avoiding them where legally possible is best of all. *Page 157*

The average since they started taking taxes in 1913 is 58.06%. *Page 163*

The reality is that you are responsible for your financial future *Pate 168*

College costs double every decade and triples in the 17 years from birth to college enrollment. *Page 169*

The very fact that you can't pay for the expense with monthly cash flow requires you to come up with a plan to finance it. *Page 181*

You never want to drain a future Savings or Investment Tank using a Future Lifestyle asset to pay for a Current Lifestyle expense. *Page 181*

Feed your tanks, finance your lifestyle. *Page 182*

Guard your collateral capacity and finance your lifestyle. *Page 182*

Self-financing takes extreme discipline. *Page 183*

Draining an asset for a Current Lifestyle expense should be your last resort. *Page 183*

Draining an account that is earning you interest has a cost. *Page 187*

Remember that draining a tank to pay cash is financing – it is self-financing. *Page 188*

Higher return potential usually comes with less control and less accessibility. *Page 188*

Borrowing with no collateral except for money you have yet to earn is the very definition of debt. *Page 189*

When you borrow and you have the capability to pay you are not in debt but you do have a liability. *Page 189*

Assets in the investment tank do not normally allow for you to borrow against them you must sell them to gain access. *Page 191*

Forget the penalty for getting out you need to know the penalty for staying in. *Page 196*

If you can qualify for one, it would be a good idea to have in place even though you have no need for the money today. *Page 200*

Accounts in the Investment Tank have the potential for greater returns but offer few benefits. Accounts in the Safe Tank offer less return potential but a greater amount of benefits. *Page 204*

If what you thought to be true turned out not to be true, when would you want to know? *Page 205*

It is important that you understand than NO life insurance contract can be considered an investment. *Page 206*

Maxwell House coffee can. *Page 206*

You should understand that it is impossible to leave someone rich through the proceeds of a life insurance contract. *Page 213*

Our minds seem to think more clearly in times of crisis than in times of comfort *Page 213*

You do not borrow "from" your policy but "against" it. *Page 214*

Key point to remember: You are earning interest on borrowed as well as non-borrowed money in a permanent life insurance policy. *Page 214*